I Want to Trust You, but I Don't

MOVING FORWARD WHEN YOU'RE SKEPTICAL OF
OTHERS, AFRAID OF WHAT GOD WILL ALLOW, AND
DOUBTFUL OF YOUR OWN DISCERNMENT

BIBLE STUDY GUIDE + STREAMING VIDEO

SIX SESSIONS

Lysa TerKeurst

#1 *NEW YORK TIMES* BESTSELLING AUTHOR

Harper*Christian*
Resources

I Want to Trust You, but I Don't Bible Study Guide
© 2024 by Lysa TerKeurst

Published in Grand Rapids, Michigan, by HarperChristian Resources. HarperChristian Resources is a registered trademark of HarperCollins Christian Publishing, Inc.

Requests for information should be sent to customercare@harpercollins.com.

ISBN 978-0-310-14570-7 (softcover)
ISBN 978-0-310-14571-4 (ebook)

HarperChristian Resources titles may be purchased in bulk for church, business, fundraising, or ministry use. For information, please e-mail ResourceSpecialist@ChurchSource.com.

First Printing August 2024 / Printed in the United States of America

Contents

Letter from Lysa

Hi friend,

Thank you for joining me to do this study about trust. I understand that you're bringing the most fragile pieces of your heart to these pages, and I want you to know . . . I am too. But I also want you to know this is a safe place to ask questions, process your skepticisms, and let the tears flow.

As I've walked through some deep relational heartbreaks over the last few years, I've come to the realization that none of us get to live this life unmarked by hurt. So none of us get to live this life without trust issues. Maybe that makes you feel comforted. Maybe that makes you feel unnerved. This will be a tension to manage, not a problem to solve. As humans, we are made for connection. But connection always comes with risk. And having the right tools to better navigate this is what so many of us have been missing in order to move forward.

That's why I wrote my book *I Want to Trust You, but I Don't* and this accompanying Bible study.

I understand the cycle of having your trust broken, then struggling to trust again, and how that can taint the way you see every other relationship in your life. But there is hope. God has shown me how important it is to use scriptural truths, self-reflection, honest assessments of relationships, and has given me a fresh look at why He is completely trustworthy. Throughout our time together, I'll share what I've learned through thousands of hours of studying the Bible and gaining wisdom from trusted friends and experts.

The good news is there are solid principles in Scripture that can help you navigate relationships with other people, God, and even yourself. And it is absolutely possible to attach your trust to a secure place that will never waver.

I know this journey may feel scary, vulnerable, or even impossible at times. But I will be with you for every part of these six sessions so we can step into our next season whole, healed, and ready to try trusting again.

Oh friend . . . we may never fully understand the twists and turns of life on this side of eternity. But I am so grateful that when everything else feels uncertain, the goodness and trustworthiness of God is something we can count on.

Now, let's go learn a thing or two about trust . . . together.

LOVE,

How To Use This Study Guide

GROUP SIZE

The *I Want to Trust You, but I Don't* video study is designed to be experienced in a group setting where meaningful discussions can take place. This could be a Bible study, a Sunday school class, or any small group gathering. To facilitate greater participation, larger groups can split up into smaller circles of four to six people after the teaching video is viewed. If you do move into smaller groups, be sure to select one person in each group to act as the facilitator during the discussion time.

MATERIALS NEEDED

To gain the most from this study, each participant should have their own copy of this study guide, as well as their own copy of the book *I Want to Trust You, but I Don't*. This study guide contains notes from the video teachings, discussion questions, and personal study days that will deepen the learning between group sessions. Additionally, the leader will need to have the videos either on DVD or by digital stream/download. This study guide also provides streaming access to the six teaching videos from Lysa.

WEEKLY SCHEDULE

At the beginning of each week, this study guide provides information on which chapters of the book should be read prior to the next group meeting. Each personal study day will lead you deeper into the biblical content of the video or book. Please note: It is recommended that participants read the introduction and chapter 1 before the first group session. On the next page is a sample of the schedule you will find at the beginning of every new week.

BEFORE GROUP MEETING	Read chapters _____ in the *I Want to Trust You, but I Don't* book.
DURING GROUP MEETING	Watch teaching video for Session _____. Group discussion will follow pages _____.
PERSONAL STUDY DAY 1	Pages _____.
PERSONAL STUDY DAY 2	Pages _____.
PERSONAL STUDY DAY 3	Pages _____.
PERSONAL STUDY DAYS 4 & 5	Read chapters _____ in the *I Want to Trust You, but I Don't* book. Complete any unfinished Personal Study activities.

TIMING

Time notations have been given for each heading of the group meeting sections of the study. These indicate the *actual* time of the video segments and the *suggested* times for discussion.

Noting these times will help you as you plan your sessions according to your individual meetings. For instance, if your group meets for two hours, you will likely have enough time to cover most of the questions, and you are welcome to use any extra time to discuss some of the previous week's homework together. Or, if your group meets for 90 minutes, you may need to select which questions you feel will draw your participants into the fullness of the group discussion. Our main goal isn't to "cover" every single question but to have deeply beneficial discussion times. In our experience, we've learned that some of the most profound moments in a Bible study occur when participants share their own experiential wisdom with one another.

Your group may opt to devote two meetings rather than one to each session. This option allows conversations to explore the content of both the study guide and the book more fully. While the first meeting could be devoted to watching the teaching video and responding to the group questions, the second meeting could be devoted to exploring the insights gained from the personal study days.

FACILITATION

Having a facilitator for each group helps in numerous ways. A facilitator is responsible for starting the video teachings. Plus, a facilitator can also read the questions aloud, encourage participation, and help keep track of time. A brief leader's guide for each session can be found in the back of this study guide.

Trust
is the
oxygen
of all
human
relationships.

Schedule

SESSION 1

BEFORE THE FIRST GROUP GATHERING	Read the introduction and chapter 1 in the *I Want to Trust You, but I Don't* book.
FIRST GROUP GATHERING	Watch Video Session 1 Group Discussion Pages 12–21
PERSONAL STUDY DAY 1	Study guide pages 22–27
PERSONAL STUDY DAY 2	Study guide pages 28–32
PERSONAL STUDY DAY 3	Study guide pages 33–40
PERSONAL STUDY DAYS 4 & 5	Read chapters 2–3 in the *I Want to Trust You, but I Don't* book.

Session 1

The Requirements
for Trust

WELCOME AND OPENING REFLECTION:
(Suggested time: 15–20 minutes)

Welcome to Session 1 of *I Want to Trust You, but I Don't.* If this is your first time gathering as a group, take a moment to introduce yourselves to the group before watching the teaching video.

Leader Note: Before starting the video, have group members share their responses to either of these questions:

What are you most looking forward to as you begin this study?

What was a helpful takeaway from the introduction or chapter 1 of the book?

VIDEO:
(Run time: 24 minutes)

Leader Note: Play the teaching video for Session 1.

As you watch the video, use the outline below to help you follow along with the teaching and to take additional notes on anything that stands out to you.

Instead of shaming ourselves for trust issues or feeling ridiculous . . . we need to recognize that our trust issues have roots in reality.

> ## Three crucial aspects that can indicate trust issues:
>
> 1. SKEPTICISM OF OTHERS
>
> 2. WHEN WE'RE TEMPTED TO BLAME GOD FOR THINGS WE DON'T UNDERSTAND
>
> 3. WHEN ANOTHER PERSON'S DECEPTIONS MAKE US DOUBT OUR OWN DISCERNMENT

Trust issues happen:

- *Horizontally* within human-to-human relationships.

- *Vertically* when we are confused by what God allowed.

- *Internally* when we aren't sure if what we are feeling is discernment or triggers from past pain.

Trust is the oxygen of all human relationships.

Trust requires two crucial factors: safety and connection.

Sin has tainted God's intention for connection and love.

Part of how trust is built in a relationship is when the connection is safe for both people.

Safety must be present in three arenas: physical, emotional, and spiritual.

> Now I urge you, brothers and sisters, to watch out for those who create divisions and obstacles contrary to the teaching that you learned. Avoid them, because such people do not serve our Lord Christ but their own appetites. They deceive the hearts of the unsuspecting with smooth talk and flattering words.
>
> **ROMANS 16:17–18 (CSB)**

Authentic relationships require vulnerability and risk.

The Hebrew word *batah* is often translated into our English Bibles as "trustworthy."

- In the Bible, when the object of trust is Yahweh/God, there is always a positive context.

- When humans are the object of trust, the majority of instances of *batah* have a negative context.

The Bible frames the concept of trust in such a way that we should always be reminded that God is the only One who is truly trustworthy.

If we want to see how safety and connection play out in a healthy way, it's this: seeking each other's highest good.

> "Dear friends, let us love one another, for love comes from God. Everyone who loves has been born of God and knows God."
>
> **1 JOHN 4:7**

When love turns from being focused on seeking the other person's highest good to becoming selfish and self-seeking, safety and connection start to get compromised, and trust soon erodes.

. . . the English phrase *one another* actually comes from a Greek reciprocal pronoun *allelous*. The focus of the love is actually reciprocity.

> This is love: not that we loved God, but that he loved us and
> sent his Son as an atoning sacrifice for our sins. Dear friends,
> since God so loved us, we also ought to love one another.
>
> 1 JOHN 4:10–11

We have a command to "love one another," but we have to be careful that we don't see this command to love as a demand to trust no matter what.

Trust is earned, not unconditionally given.

In order for trust to be present, the requirements of trust must be established, accepted, and lived out.

Group Discussion

(SUGGESTED TIME 40–45 MINUTES)

Leader Note: The ultimate goal for this time together is to have a meaningful discussion with others as you draw closer to God. The following suggested questions are designed to guide you into and through a rich discussion time together. Feel free to add your own questions to this list, or remove questions that don't seem like a good fit.

SUGGESTED QUESTIONS . . .

1. In the introduction video, Lysa observed that we often place more trust in people we *don't* know than in people we *do*. She gave a few examples, such as flying in an airplane or hiring a rideshare.

    Let's start our time together by reading what the Bible says about trusting someone or something more than God. How can we apply this timeless wisdom to our lives today?

    Psalm 146:1–6

    Psalm 20:7

2. Please open your Bibles and have one person read Deuteronomy 7:7–9 aloud. What do these verses tell us about the character of God? What other ways do we know God is trustworthy? Your examples could come from the Bible or your personal experience.

3. Lysa shared a sentence that resonated with her for years: "Trust is the oxygen of all human relationships." How do you define trust?

4. There are two requirements of trust: safety and connection. What are some behaviors that occur when a healthy connection is made between two people? What behaviors can occur when safety and connection aren't there?

5. In the video we learned that safety must be present in three arenas: physical, emotional, and spiritual. Read the following verses and discuss how Jesus modeled safety, keeping in mind Lysa's definitions.

   John 8:2–11 (physical and spiritual)
   Mark 4:35–41 (physical)
   John 11:32–35 (emotional)
   John 5:19–20 (emotional and spiritual)

Definitions of the three arenas where trust can be broken:

Physical

IN ADDITION TO PHYSICAL HARM, A LACK OF PHYSICAL SAFETY CAN INCLUDE WHEN SOMEONE IS DISMISSIVE OVER YOUR CONCERNS OR THERE'S A LACK OF PROTECTION. (FOR MORE ON PHYSICAL SAFETY, SEE THE NOTES ON ABUSE IN THE BACK OF THE GUIDE IN PAGES 200–202.)

Emotional

THIS CAN INCLUDE THREATENING, YELLING, OR INTENTIONALLY MAKING SOMEONE FEEL AFRAID OR BELITTLED. IT CAN ALSO INCLUDE HARMFUL DISCLOSURES OF CONFIDENTIAL INFORMATION, DISLOYALTY, INFIDELITY, AND DISHONESTY.

Spiritual

WHEN SCRIPTURE IS USED AS A WEAPON OR A MANIPULATION TACTIC TO GAIN CONTROL, KEEP POWER OVER SOMEONE, OR DISREGARD THE OTHER PERSON'S PERSONAL DIGNITY AND VALUE AS A SON OR DAUGHTER OF GOD.

6. Read Lysa's definition of how spiritual safety can be broken. Next read Romans 16:17–18 (CSB) aloud: *Now I urge you, brothers and sisters, to watch out for those who create divisions and obstacles contrary to the teaching that you learned. Avoid them, because such people do not serve our Lord Christ but their own appetites. They deceive the hearts of the unsuspecting with smooth talk and flattering words.*

The apostle Paul knew the potential for falsehood and division within the church and ended the letter to the Romans with this final warning. What are some ways believers can provide spiritual safety for each other?

7. Read 1 John 4:7: *Dear friends, let us love one another, for love comes from God. Everyone who loves has been born of God and knows God.* In the video, you learned that the English phrase "one another" actually comes from a Greek reciprocal pronoun *allelous*. This conveys that love between two people should bounce back and forth with equal weight and value. Share examples of what this type of love looks like between people in various situations.

8. To end our time together, share any thoughts you have after watching the video and having our discussion. Did anything surprise you? Challenge you? Or give you something to work on in the next week?

CLOSING:
(Suggested time: 5 minutes)

Leader Note: Read the following instructions and clarify any questions your group may have about the homework and what each participant should do between now and the next session. Then, take a few minutes to pray with your group. You can use the prayer provided on the following page or pray your own prayer.

BEFORE THE NEXT SESSION . . .

Every week, the *I Want to Trust You, but I Don't Study Guide* includes five days of personal study to help you draw closer to God and His Word. For the first week of personal study, you'll work with the video session, as well as the introduction and chapter 1 of *I Want to Trust You, but I Don't* book. You'll also have time to read chapters 2–3 of the book in preparation for our next time together.

PRAYER

Lord, thank You for being so trustworthy in a world where it can be hard to trust people. Forgive us for the times we have doubted You because of how someone else has treated us. You have never let Your people down in the past, and we trust You with everything we face today. We ask You to guide us through this study and show us the ways You want to bring healing to our hearts and lives. In Jesus' name, Amen.

Personal Study

Today we'll focus on Session 1 of the *I Want to Trust You, but I Don't* video series. If you haven't already watched it, please do so before you begin.

Welcome to the first day of your personal study in this six-session study of *I Want to Trust You, but I Don't*. I'm so glad you decided to join me as we work through the hardships of trust issues with others, ourselves, and God.

As you watch the teaching videos and read the book, you'll likely hear or read something that touches a tender place in your heart. We all have various forms of trust issues because we've spent our lives interacting with other humans, and humans are prone to making hurtful, selfish choices.

I want you to know that whether you were hurt years ago or you are walking through a confusing and hurtful situation right now, I understand.

I've dealt with broken trust in the past, and just when I think I've made progress in moving forward, a word or memory can trigger the pain, and the wounds feel raw.

But I also know that healing is possible with God's help. Ultimately, my hope for you is that you'll regain the confidence that God is completely trustworthy. If we truly believe this, then we won't be so afraid of what will happen to us when others break our trust.

1. In the introduction video, I shared a story about my daughter making a checklist of her concerns about sleepovers. The concerns on her checklist were valid—they were based on past experiences. It's important to recognize that trust issues are rooted in reality.

We probably all have had an experience where we said, "I'll never do that again!" If you've said that or something similar, write down what happened and what might be on your checklist.

2. There are three ways trust issues can happen:

    - *Horizontally* within human-to-human relationships.

    - *Vertically* when we are confused by what God allowed, which makes us fearful of our future.

    - *Internally* when we aren't sure if what we are feeling is discernment or really triggers from past pain.

    As you think about these three ways, which way have you experienced trust issues in more than the others? In a few sentences, summarize what you are thinking and feeling about trust in this area.

3. If you seek safety and connection, you aren't alone. God wired us to desire these two conditions. However, when someone we love no longer feels safe because they've broken our trust in life-altering ways, we can start to wonder why God is allowing this. It can be easy to think God has forgotten us or, worse, that He doesn't care. I've wrestled with these thoughts too. But that's when we remind ourselves that God is absolutely trustworthy and His character doesn't change. Read the following verses and identify how God is trustworthy and protects His children:

    Numbers 23:19

Psalm 91:4

Matthew 6:26

Ephesians 6:10–18

2 Timothy 3:16–17

4. Even though God is completely trustworthy, we won't always understand why He allows hard things to happen. When our trust in Him is shaken, we might wrongly shift our confidence to the things of this world to meet our needs. The problem is we instinctively know people and things can let us down. They can't be our ultimate anchor for stability. So we can find ourselves insecure, anxious, and fearful.

Take some time to consider where you might have placed your trust in things other than God. Here's an example to get you started:

I'm worried I might get laid off at my job because they are downsizing. I'm trusting my employer to be my provider instead of God.

I'm afraid of _____. I'm trusting _____ instead of God.

I'm nervous about _____. Maybe I'm trusting _____ to _____ rather than God.

5. Now that you've identified some areas of misplaced trust, rewrite the sentences above to declare your reassignment. For example, *Lord, I trust You as my provider, not my employer.* Use these declaration sentences as a restatement of biblical truth.

    Lord, I put my trust in You for _____, not _____.

    Lord, I place my confidence in You for _____, not _____.

6. Now, let's spend some more time looking at the Hebrew word *batah,* which is often translated as "trustworthy" in our English Bibles. Remember, in the Bible, when the object of trust is Yahweh/God, there is always a positive context to it. Our circumstances and our understanding of what's happening to us may feel risky, but God's character contains no risk. He is always trustworthy.

    However, when humans are the object of trust, the majority of instances of *batah* have a negative context. The Bible frames the concept of trust so that we should always be reminded that God is the only One who is truly trustworthy.

    Read the following verses and write the action, result, or reason connected with trusting in the Lord.

    Psalm 4:5

    Psalm 37:3

    Psalm 62:8

    Proverbs 3:5

    Isaiah 26:4

Which of these verses speak to you most personally and why?

The following are examples of trusting in something or someone other than God. Read the following verses and identify the warning or object of misplaced trust.

Psalm 41:9

Psalm 146:3

Isaiah 31:1

Psalm 49:6

Which of these verses speak to you most personally and why?

7. Consider this statement from the Session 1 video: "We have a command to 'love one another,' but we have to be careful that we don't see this command to love as a demand to trust no matter what." If you are in a relationship with someone you love, but your trust in them has been damaged, how can you continue to love well while being wise and guarding your heart? (For example, you might need to stop following them on social media because it's not good for you to see what they're doing all the time. Or, you might need to limit the topics you talk to them about.)

We've come to the end of Day 1. And it's possible this study is stirring up some pain in your heart. If that's true for you, can I whisper some reassurance to you? I have resisted moving forward because of the pain too. No one wants to relive pain. But you aren't doing it alone.

We have a God who promises to be so very present in our circumstances. As we end this day of study, take a few moments to talk to God about where you are right now. Be honest with every fear, worry, and hurt. Feel free to use the space below to write down your prayer if you like. And then, take a deep breath and commit to showing up tomorrow to continue your healing.

Today we are reflecting on the Introduction in the *I Want to Trust You, but I Don't* book. Please take some time to read it, if you haven't already.

Dealing with trust issues can be exhausting. I've wrestled with this for years . . . feeling hopeful that someone will do what they say they'll do, be where they say they'll be, and tell me the truth even though it might be hard or embarrassing. And sometimes this happens. When it does, my confidence in that person grows and strengthens.

But other times, when a person lets me down or, worse, betrays me, I'm disappointed, hurt, and suspicious. This is true not just for the person who let me down, but a feeling of mistrust can spread under the surface and infect even my healthy relationships.

The road to healing took years of prayer, counseling, and lots of inner work. But with God's help, I kept going. I kept trying. I made progress. And I know you can too.

In this process, I learned we all have trust issues at some level. We've all been let down by someone; we've all been hurt. I hope that truth makes you feel less alone in your pain. If I could, I'd sit down next to you and listen to your story. But since that's not possible today, I hope the words in the pages of my book and this study will bring comfort to you.

In the introduction of the book, I shared how exhausting it has been to work through friendship breakups, abandonment from people I thought would stick by me, betrayals of the deepest kind, and all the grief and emotional turmoil that followed.

Fear of getting hurt again and being suspicious of even the safe people in my life made me want to isolate. Or I would try to control interactions, hoping this would protect me. I wanted to be able to trust some people, but fear had such a loud voice.

1. How have you experienced the negative role that fear can play in your relationships with others?

It's normal to have fear when we've been hurt. Throughout this book, you will find that I empathize deeply with your fear. Fear is a God-given response to keep us safe. Yet, when I read the Bible, I find that many times, God told His children not to be afraid. It's not that God didn't care about their fear; it's just that He didn't want the spirit of fear to imprison them and keep them from being obedient to Him.

After all, no person is more powerful than God. No matter what we walk through, no person has the ability to thwart God's good plan for us.

2. We may not understand the heartbreaks we experience, but we can weather them better if we have the solid foundation that trusting God is safe and He will help us. How have you experienced this?

This was sometimes hard for me to believe when I was walking through the death of my marriage. But now that years have passed, I can look back and see how God helped me even though I could not understand it at the time.

Through this study, we will work on learning to trust the right people and appropriately distrust those who are not worthy of our trust. But ultimately, we are anchoring our hope in the Lord to lead us, teach us, guide us, and heal us.

3. In each of these verses, God tells His people not to be afraid. Identify the reason God gave to show them why they didn't need to fear.

    Genesis 26:23–24

    Genesis 46:3–4

Joshua 1:9

Deuteronomy 1:29–31

4. These were promises personally made for these situations, but the principle of God being with His people very much applies to us, even if it plays out in different ways. How does this understanding of God's presence make a difference in your life? In your relationships?

5. When we are unsure of who to trust, we can make negative assumptions about people's words and choices. These suspicions can be hard to process and can result in us responding in ways that don't reflect our true selves. Read this quote from the book, then answer the following questions.

> "Sometimes, what we are sensing is spot on and helps us know what needs to be addressed. But other times we are unnecessarily projecting things onto others that just aren't there. We don't want to get it wrong, but we also don't know what to do from here. These kinds of mental gymnastics are exhausting and make us hold back the very best of who we are for fear of getting hurt." (p. xvi)

- How have "mental gymnastics" held you back from being your very best?

- Can you identify ways your personality has changed from your past hurt? Is there something you can do differently this next week to start to reclaim that beautiful part of yourself?

I ended the book's introduction by sharing how a SPECT brain scan showed physical evidence of my past trauma. It wasn't all an emotional issue, but my brain had been impacted, which explained the changes in my processing.

This obviously didn't surprise God. He knows that trauma affects how we think and our ability to trust Him and other people.

We see God's kindness in how He dealt with the Israelites after He freed them from the harsh and cruel treatment of the Egyptians for four hundred years (Genesis 15:13, Acts 7:6). God's people suffered trauma—physical, mental, and emotional abuse for generations. So, part of God's plan for freedom was to reset their minds from distrust to trust.

The Old Testament book of Exodus recounts the miraculous story of Moses and the freeing of the Israelites. But I want us to move past the plagues and the parting of the Red Sea to the Israelites in the wilderness and how God started to build trust between Himself and His people.

Read Exodus 16:11–23. In verse 23, God asked the Israelites to take a day of rest and to trust they would have enough food gathered from the previous day to sustain them.

6. From God's perspective, how might this command for a day of rest help to build trust?

7. We know God wanted His people to trust Him, but how might they have misinterpreted God's command given their past trauma?

Read the words of Jesus, recorded thousands of years later in Matthew 11:28–30:

> "Come to me, all you who are weary and burdened, and I will give you rest. Take my yoke upon you and learn from me, for I am gentle and humble in heart, and you will find rest for your souls. For my yoke is easy and my burden is light."

8. How do your heart and soul respond to this gentle and loving invitation?

9. In verse 29, what kind of rest does Jesus offer? How might this rest be different from physical rest?

God's first command of His people was to rest, and then Jesus invites *us* to rest. While God's rest involves a physical break, it's so much more. My soul breathes most deeply when at rest and assured of God's love, presence, and protection. This is both an invitation and a promise for those of us who are exhausted from the sin of this world.

As we end this day's study, soak in the truth of the words from Jesus in Matthew 11:28–30. And remember that the trauma of having your trust broken by people you thought would never betray you can be life-altering. But it doesn't have to be life-ruining.

Today we'll reflect on chapter 1 of the *I Want to Trust You, but I Don't* book.
If you haven't already read chapter 1, please do so before we begin.

Welcome to Day 3 of our study on trust. I pray that in our first few days together, you are already feeling less alone in your experience of having your trust broken. Although the details surrounding your experience may be different from mine, I imagine we share some similar feelings in response to the pain.

And maybe you've experienced the disappointing feelings I wrote about in the first chapter, when hope started to feel like a setup for more disappointment. The Bible even addresses this. Proverbs 13:12 says, *Hope deferred makes the heart sick . . .*

I know that sinking feeling when you want things to change, but past experience tells you that it's unlikely things will improve.

Hope is a risky pursuit when your trust is broken. Relationships can seem so unpredictable and sometimes undependable. Daring to hope things will change can feel like walking on thin ice over a frozen pond. You never quite feel secure and the only thing you are confident in is that one wrong step will plunge you into painfully cold waters.

In your head you don't want to live that pessimistic way, but your heart screams "Danger!" when you start to hope again.

And yet . . . what we see with our eyes isn't the whole picture. The Bible tells us there is always more going on than we can see. God is always present and always working. The hard part for our human understanding is *how* He works and how *long* it will take.

In our time together today, I want to gently invite you to shift your perspective about your situation. Instead of declaring the worst will happen, I want to challenge us both to stop and say, *But what if some parts of this do work out?* It's in that little question that something can start to shift in our hearts.

So, let's start today's study with an assessment (on a scale of 1–5) of your hope level. Acknowledging reality is the best way to face your fears and move toward hope.

1. Think about these areas of your life and consider your hope level in each, with 1 being the lowest. A ranking of 1 might mean you've given up hope that things will ever change in this area.

   A 5 ranking would be an area where you have great hope. Maybe this is an area where your heart feels safe and secure. I've left some blanks for you to customize this assessment.

AREA OF LIFE	1	2	3	4	5
FRIENDSHIPS					
EXTENDED FAMILY RELATIONSHIPS					
ROMANTIC RELATIONSHIP/ MARRIAGE					
CHILDREN					
MINISTRY WORK					
CHURCH					
JOB OR CAREER					
PHYSICAL HEALING					
MENTAL HEALTH					
RELATIONSHIP WITH GOD					

Giving up hope can feel so logical when we've been disappointed over and over. Hope can feel fragile. And when our emotions are raw, putting ourselves out there can just seem too risky. The danger of this self-protection is we can transfer that lack of hope in people to God. We assume He'll abandon us like others have. Or He'll answer other people's prayers, but not ours. We've all had these thoughts. But sometimes our doubts and uncertainties can spiral until they affect our faith.

2. What changes do you see in your routines, habits, or thought processes when a lack of hope in God starts to work its way into your life?

What we see with our human eyes is absolutely real. But if we only focus on what our physical eyes can see, we will miss what is happening in the supernatural realm.

There's a fascinating story found in 2 Kings 6:8–17 that should encourage us. It shows that what we see with our eyes isn't evidence of God's action or inaction. And knowing there's an entire other story happening can help to shift our perspective when we feel hopeless.

Here's a summary of the story. Elisha succeeded Elijah in the office of the prophet of Israel. As part of his role, Elisha warned the king of Israel about the movements of an enemy king (Aram). When King Aram found out, he was enraged and sought to capture Elisha with the Aramean armies.

Imagine the scene that morning when Elisha and his servant awoke to find an army surrounding the city. Read 2 Kings 6:15–17 to see what happened.

3. How do you relate to this story of circumstances seeming impossible to overcome?

4. What was the servant's response to what he could see with his eyes?

5. After Elisha prayed, what did God reveal was happening in the spiritual realm?

6. How does this story offer you comfort when you are feeling hopeless about your situation?

This is just one example in Scripture of God working behind the scenes to protect His people. That's why when we talk about hope, it's important to remind ourselves of the source.

In this psalm of ascent, which we could think of today as a song of remembrance, the focus is on the source of true hope: *Israel, put your hope in the LORD, for with the LORD is unfailing love and with him is full redemption* (Psalm 130:7–8).

Where hope gets risky is when we place it in the wrong things. In the book I wrote:

> "Hope is either the most beautiful feeling of possibility or it's the worst feeling of defeat. To dare to hope is to simultaneously expose our greatest desires and our greatest fears. But if we're not willing to risk hoping, then we are already quietly quitting on a better future." (p. 3)

If your hope level is low today and your despair level is high, I want to encourage you with the idea that you can reignite hope. But I don't think we can just will our hearts to change. It isn't an issue of self-control. It is an issue of having the right foundation for hope.

So we have to take a few steps back before we can hope again. Let's start with some definitions of trust, faith, and hope.

Trust: The confident reliance on the character, ability, strength, or truth of someone or something. Scripture affirms the total trustworthiness of God, especially in relation to His promises to His people.[1]

Faith: The persuasion of the mind that a certain statement is true.[2] The Greek word translated "faith" is *pistis* and it reflects both a mental commitment and then behavior in alignment with that commitment.

Hope: An expectation or belief in the fulfillment of something desired.[3]

As we look at these definitions, there seems to be a progression. First we trust, and as we are learning in this book, trust is built on a track record of dependability.

Then, once we have trust, we have faith that a person is worthy of our trust.

Finally, once we've experienced trust, our faith is grounded, and then we can hope.

7. Sometimes, hope is the result of other conditions. We don't just naturally drift into hope. We base our hope on who or what has proven trustworthy. Take some time to record evidence of God's faithfulness in your life, to remind yourself of why you can trust Him.

To see another example of a progression to hope, read Romans 5:1–5.

---

1 *Merriam-Webster's Collegiate Dictionary*, 11th ed., s.v. "trust."

2 M. G. Easton, *Illustrated Bible Dictionary and Treasury of Biblical History, Biography, Geography, Doctrine, and Literature*, rev. ed., (London: T. Nelson and Sons, 1894), 250.

3 Paul K. McAlister, "Hope," in *Baker Encyclopedia of the Bible*, vol. 1, ed. Walter A. Elwell (Grand Rapids: Baker, 1988), 996:

8. Write down the conditions that lead to hope in these verses. On the surface, these conditions wouldn't naturally lead to hope. What are some reasons that suffering might lead to hope if we process it rightly?

> We wait in hope for the LORD; he is our help and our shield. In him our hearts rejoice, for we trust in his holy name. May your unfailing love be with us, LORD, even as we put our hope in you.
>
> **PSALM 33:20–22**

I ended this chapter with a description of what compassionate processing looks like. Too many of us have blamed ourselves when others let us down . . . if only we'd been more aware, or made a different decision. But no one can go back in time and change anything. We can only be thankful for what we've learned today and use that knowledge wisely in the future.

Compassionate Statements

I'm going to be honest with myself and stay committed to reality throughout this process. I won't sugarcoat or make things look better than they are.

I will not take responsibility for or try to fix other people. I will own only what is mine to own.

I will be compassionate toward myself, realizing that when you know better, you do better. The fact that I picked up this book shows that I want to know better so that I can do better.

Instead of shaming myself for not picking up on the red flags in previous relationships sooner, I'm going to choose to feel appropriately convicted to make better choices in the future. I'm not going to believe the lie that it's too late to change.

I will acknowledge that I'm a victim of hurt, but I'm not going to live as a victim. I am now going to be empowered to take charge of my own healing.

I still believe there's a beautiful world with wonderful people to connect with, to laugh with, to dance with, to explore with, to live with, and to have purpose and make a difference with.

I am now willing to learn how to trust my own discernment again, how to appropriately trust the right people, and how to trust God even when I don't understand what He's doing.

9. Of the seven compassion statements at the end of chapter 1, and included in today's study, which one resonates with you the most, and why?

Finish your personal study today by asking for God's help to move forward this week with compassion and love for yourself and others.

DAYS 4 & 5

Read chapters 2 and 3.

Use these days to go back and complete any of the reflection questions or activities from the previous days this week that you weren't able to finish. Make note of any revelations you've had and reflect on any growth or personal insights you've gained.

Spend the next two days reading chapters 2 and 3 of the book *I Want to Trust You, but I Don't.* Use the space below to note anything in the chapters that stands out to you or encourages your heart.

Schedule

BEFORE YOUR GROUP GATHERING	Read chapters 2–3 in the *I Want to Trust You, but I Don't* book.
GROUP GATHERING	Watch Video Session 2 Group Discussion Pages 44–52
PERSONAL STUDY DAY 1	Study guide pages 53–57
PERSONAL STUDY DAY 2	Study guide pages 58–62
PERSONAL STUDY DAY 3	Study guide pages 63–69
PERSONAL STUDY DAYS 4 & 5	Read chapters 4–5 in the *I Want to Trust You, but I Don't* book.

Do They Value Trust Like You Do?

WELCOME AND OPENING REFLECTION:

(Suggested time: 15–20 minutes)

Welcome to Session 2 of *I Want to Trust You, but I Don't.*

Leader Note: Before starting the video, take a few moments to check in with your group about how they are doing. Let the group warm up a bit by asking if there was anything from their personal study time they'd like to share with the group.

VIDEO:

(Run time: 18 minutes)

Leader Note: Play the teaching video for Session 2.

As you watch the video, use the outline below to help you follow along with the teaching and to take additional notes on anything that stands out to you.

When we don't know what to look for, we'll miss what we need to see.

Red flags are like smoke . . . "Where there's smoke there is a fire."

Red Flag #1: Incongruity
When someone's actions don't line up with who they say they are.

Red Flag #2: Inconsistency
When someone is unpredictable.

Red Flag #3: Insincerity
When someone tells you something they think you want to hear, but they don't actually mean it.

Red Flag #4: Self-Centeredness
When someone doesn't think about how their words and actions impact other people.

Red Flag #5: Insecurity
When someone has a struggle inside of them they expect you to fix.

Red Flag #6: Immaturity
When someone acts emotionally or spiritually undeveloped, juvenile, or childish.

Red Flag #7: Immorality
When someone has a disregard for the principles of right and wrong.

Red Flag #8: Insubordination
When someone rejects and is disobedient to good and reasonable authority.

Red Flag #9: Incompetence
When someone says they are capable of doing something they don't have the training, ability, experience, or track record to carry out.

Red Flag #10: Irresponsibility
When someone doesn't prioritize tasks that are really important.

Red Flag #11: Inflated Sense of Self
When someone thinks they are so good or important that you could not manage without them.

Does a person's pattern of thinking and resulting actions indicate their mind is set on things that honor or dishonor God?

A person's mindset reveals what they long for, desire, and put action to. In a relationship, both people's mindsets need to be congruent; otherwise, trust will be eroded, because what you value in the relationship will be different than what they value in the relationship.

It does not honor God for someone to act dishonorably.

Mindset in Greek is *phronema*—meaning, to take someone's side.

Questions to ask yourself in a relationship:

- What does this person value?

- Do they value trust in a relationship like you do?

- Do their values for a relationship line up with what you value for a relationship?

Where there are differences in what you value, that can often be the birthplace for distrust.

You have two choices: you can either work together to better align what you value and desire in the relationship or be willing to run the risk of continued broken trust.

Where there are constant red flag behaviors, there will be a lack of trust and therefore a lack of peace.

> Let the peace of Christ rule in your hearts, since as members of one body you were called to peace. And be thankful.
>
> COLOSSIANS 3:15

In order for "peace" to rule in our hearts we have to have relationships with others that are built on trust and consistency of character marked by integrity.

Group Discussion

Leader Note: We have included some questions to get your group discussion started. Feel free to add your own or modify what's here. The goal is for your group to have a meaningful discussion.

1. Having healthy relationships will help bring us peace. Thankfully, the Bible gives us many examples of what relationships should and shouldn't look like. Read the following verses aloud and identify what the Bible instructs us about the ways people should and should not treat one another.

    - Matthew 7:12

    - 1 Corinthians 13:6–7

    - Romans 13:8–10

    - Colossians 3:12–23

2. Read Matthew 7:1–3. We need to be careful as we look at red flags not to slip into judging people on the whole of their character or making a final conclusion about who they are going to be without leaving room for God to work in their lives all the while being unwilling to examine our own hearts. For example, just because someone shows some behaviors on the red flag list does not mean that they can't be a good friend or that they aren't walking with the Lord. We all have struggles. Remember, we must look at the severity and how often these red flags present themselves.

    Why is this reminder important in a specific situation you are facing right now?

Why is it crucial to examine our own hearts and actions in this process?

3. Lysa mentioned eleven red flags in a relationship. You can find them in the video notes for Session 2. All of these character traits are discussed in Scripture, and God has provided both warnings against them and encouragement to pursue honorable behavior.

    Take turns reading the verses below, and as a group, identify ideal elements of Christian character.

RED FLAG	SCRIPTURE REFERENCE	IDEAL ELEMENTS OF CHRISTIAN CHARACTER
INCONGRUITY	Matthew 6:24	
INCONSISTENCY	1 John 2:5-11	
INSINCERITY	1 Peter 1:22; James 3:10–12	
SELF-CENTEREDNESS	Philippians 2:2–4	
INSECURITY	Jeremiah 17:7–8	
IMMATURITY	James 1:4	
IMMORALITY	Mark 7:20–23; 1 Peter 2:11	
INSUBORDINATION	Romans 13:7; Proverbs 12:1	
INCOMPETENCE	Colossians 3:23–24	
IRRESPONSIBILITY	James 4:17; Micah 6:8	
INFLATED SENSE OF SELF	Colossians 3:12; Proverbs 28:26	

4. Navigating all relationships can be challenging. Why is it important for Christians to have accountability and support from biblically wise Christian friends and family when dealing with relationships? Read Proverbs 11:14 and James 3:13–17 for some ideas.

5. To wrap up your time together, read Colossians 3:15–17. In light of our discussion today, how do these verses encourage you or give you an action step for your life this week?

CLOSING:
(Suggested time: 5 minutes)

Leader Note: Read the following instructions and clarify any questions your group may have about the homework and what each participant should do between now and the next session. Then, take a few minutes to pray with your group. You can use the prayer provided or pray your own prayer.

BEFORE THE NEXT SESSION . . .

Every week, the *I Want to Trust You, but I Don't Study Guide* includes five days of personal study to help you make meaningful connections between your life and what you're learning each week. This week, you'll do more review of the video we discussed today, and then work through chapters 2 and 3 of the *I Want to Trust You, but I Don't* book. You'll also have time to read chapters 4 and 5 of the book in preparation for our next study together.

PRAYER

Lord, as we navigate the complexities of human relationships, we come before You seeking wisdom and discernment. Help us to recognize red flags and warning signs, and to be cautious in our interactions with those who may seek to deceive or manipulate us. And Lord, help us to see what's in our own hearts before we point the finger at others. We long to have our minds set on things of Your Spirit. Help us to turn from things of the flesh and be people who please You with our hearts and actions. In Jesus' name, Amen.

Personal Study

Today we'll focus on Session 2 of the *I Want to Trust You, but I Don't* video series. If you haven't already watched it, please do so before you begin.

In the group discussion, we reviewed red flags, but in your study today and throughout this week, we'll explore how to identify red flags in relationships and what to do about them.

An important realization I had about red flags was that I wasn't always honest with myself about how concerning these really were. Some behaviors seemed troublesome, but I also didn't want to blow them out of proportion or make them a bigger deal than I should.

The challenge for me, and I'm guessing for you, is because I believe so firmly in giving grace, there were many times I brushed off something that should have made me stop and question what I was seeing. How could I tell when someone's behavior was an isolated event or when it revealed something more concerning? After all, we all make mistakes.

That's why identifying those eleven red flags has been so helpful for me. They now give me guidance on what could be an issue to address in a relationship. And sometimes the issue might be with me. That's where I want us to start today, with looking inward before we look outward.

1. Let's personalize the concept of looking at ourselves before we look at others. Jesus said, "Why do you look at the speck of sawdust in your brother's eye and pay no attention to the plank in your own eye? . . . first take the plank out of your own eye, and then you will see clearly to remove the speck from your brother's eye" (Matthew 7:4–5).

Review the list of red flags in the video notes (pp. 45–46) and prayerfully ask God to reveal any wrong thought, word, or deed that aligns with an item on that list. Write down an area you might be struggling with here.

2. In the video, I shared the Greek word *phronema,* which is translated "mindset." There are two different mindsets: those set on the desires of the Spirit and those set on the desires of the flesh (sinful humanity). Interestingly, *phronema* also has a nuance of aspiring toward, which means not only do we choose a side, but we actively pursue the goals of that side.

Read Romans 8:5–8. Now think of men and women you have known personally or observed from a distance who reflect these two mindsets: either living with their minds on the flesh or on the Spirit.

These examples could be from the Bible, human history, or current day. Identify five actions of a person who aspires toward things of the Spirit and five actions of a person who pursues the flesh.

SPIRIT	FLESH

3. Because we all come to Jesus with a bent toward the things of the flesh, we have to work at changing our mindset to focus on the Spirit. We will never accidentally stumble into a Spirit-led mindset. This process takes time and being intentional with our choices.

Romans 12:2 gives us an insight into how this change happens:

> Do not conform to the pattern of this world, but be transformed by the renewing of your mind. Then you will be able to test and approve what God's will is—his good, pleasing and perfect will.

The phrase "be transformed" is translated from the Greek word *metamorphousthe*. The tense of the word indicates this isn't a one-and-done action, but a process. And anything we want to change requires practice.

Here are some areas where little changes can impact our minds. Even small efforts put into spiritual disciplines or wise choices will accumulate over time, eventually making a noticeable difference. What's one wise choice you can make in each of these areas this week?

PRAYER   _____

READING THE BIBLE   _____

MEMORIZING SCRIPTURE   _____

ACTIVITIES IN MY FREE TIME   _____

WHAT I LISTEN TO   _____

SPENDING TIME WITH OTHER BELIEVERS   _____

PRACTICING GRATITUDE   _____

WORSHIP   _____

4. Any time we talk about areas in our personal lives that need to change, we can easily move into feelings of regret or shame. Some regret is healthy as it leads to repentance. But we should always keep in mind that we serve a God who doesn't condemn us for our past sinful choices. As long as we are truly repentant, we aren't rejected. In fact, right before Romans 8:5–8, the apostle Paul reminds us of God's power over sin and His power in our lives.

Read Romans 8:1–4 and fill in the blanks. (The following passage is taken from the NIV.)

Romans 8:1–4
Therefore, there is now _____ for those who are in Christ Jesus, because through _____ the law of the Spirit who _____ has set you _____ from the law of sin and death. For what the law was powerless to do because it was weakened by the flesh, _____ by sending _____ in the likeness of sinful flesh to be a sin offering. And so he _____ in the flesh, in order that the righteous requirement of the law might be fully met in us, who do not live according to the flesh but _____.

5. Knowing that followers of Jesus are free from the enslaving power of sin, what difference does that make in how you face your current relationship challenges?

6. In the video, before I shared the eleven red flags, I invited you to write down any red flags you might be tripping over with the people in your life. Take the time to identify the issues that you are dealing with right now. Are these isolated events? Or is there a pattern?

7. The Bible is clear that Christians have a responsibility to each other. The idea of "live and let live" simply isn't found in the Bible. In fact, we are called to a higher level of community and commitment to each other than those who are outside the faith.

Read the next few verses and identify the action listed, as it pertains to how we should interact with other believers. Then identify how you are doing in this area on a scale of 1 to 5, with 1 meaning "I could use some growth in this area" and 5 meaning "This is an area of strength."

VERSE	ACTION(S)	MY RESPONSE
JOHN 13:34–35		1 2 3 4 5
GALATIANS 5:13		1 2 3 4 5
1 PETER 4:10		1 2 3 4 5
GALATIANS 6:1		1 2 3 4 5
GALATIANS 6:2		1 2 3 4 5
HEBREWS 10:24–25		1 2 3 4 5
MATTHEW 5:23–24		1 2 3 4 5

8. As we close this personal study day, remember this truth:

> Therefore, if anyone is in Christ, the new creation has
> come: The old has gone, the new is here!
>
> **2 CORINTHIANS 5:17**

Spend a few minutes writing a prayer of praise for the way God forgives and changes us from the inside out.

Today we are going to explore chapter 2 in the *I Want to Trust You, but I Don't* book. If you haven't already read chapter 2, please do so before you begin.

Friend, look at how far you've already come! We are in the middle of Week 2 and I'm so proud that you are committed to learning and growing in this area of trust and relationships.

We are going to look at triggers this week, but before we study what they are and how they affect us, I want us to look at the birthplace of distrust. Humankind didn't start out doubting God.

The very first traumatic event that impacted our trust in God's goodness and faithfulness happened in Genesis. It is here we can trace back to the biblical birthplace of doubting and disbelieving that God has our best interest in mind.

The Bible tells us that God made Adam and Eve and "they felt no shame" (Genesis 2:25). Life was perfect—a perfect relationship with God and each other. Then, in Genesis 3, a serpent enters the picture and asks a question about the details of God's command regarding the trees.

Most of us know how the story goes, but if you need a refresher, you can read about it in Genesis 3:1–6. And after Adam and Eve disobeyed, they became aware of their nakedness, and we can assume they felt shame because they covered themselves.

1. Read Genesis 3:8–11 and answer the following questions.

   • What happened when Adam and Eve heard God walking?

   • What was Adam's response when God called to him?

- Describe Adam and Eve's relationship with God up to that point.

- How did their experience with the serpent impact their relationship with God?

I can relate so much to Adam and Eve. Past experiences seem to profoundly impact my current relationships—not only with people but with God too.

My brain is always trying to figure out if I'm safe or not. Read this quote from the book and answer the question below.

> "... my nervous system was letting me know I was too close to a situation that had hurt me previously. And connecting these two experiences made my fear skyrocket." (p. 17)

2. Because God designed us with great intention, why would He build this kind of response to past situations into our nervous systems?

3. Let's go back to Genesis and look at how Adam and Eve continued to respond when they were afraid. Read Genesis 3:11–13.

   - What two questions did God ask?

   - What was Adam's response?

- What was Eve's response?

4. In the chapter, I discussed the process called *neuroception*. This is where our neurological makeup triggers the automatic defense strategies of fight, flight, or freeze. Looking back at the story in Genesis, identify which defense strategies we see Adam and Eve use.

5. God had proven Himself trustworthy to Adam and Eve, but their fear over what happened with the serpent caused them to treat God with suspicion and blame. As an exercise, how might Adam and Eve have responded given the trustworthiness of God?

Our earthly relationships are always with humans. And even the very best humans aren't God. So, the reality of our human experience is that we will experience a lack of trust. This is where we'll spend the rest of our time together today.

In this book I shared the truth that every trauma has two parts to it: 1) the fact of what happened and 2) the impact it had on us. The impact is what happens when a relationship situation feels risky. When we feel that risk, we have the choice to face our feelings or avoid them. As I shared in yesterday's study, I've often tried to rationalize what I was experiencing and feeling—to my own detriment.

6. What's your go-to response when you experience a relationship situation that feels risky?

If your response to pain is to avoid it, you are in good company. Many of us struggle to deal with feelings that connect us back to a painful experience. In the book, I shared four ways we avoid or dismiss our feelings. Let's look at those more deeply. For each response, read the description in the book on pages 21–25. Then, write down your experience with that response. For example, if you tend to go numb when facing hard feelings, how do you "numb out"? Or if your go-to is shame, what are some harsh statements you've spoken to yourself?

Response #1: Numb

Response #2: Ignore

Response #3: Override

Response #4: Shame

As we end our time together today, I want to affirm that having emotions and feelings doesn't mean you are weak. It's not bad to have uncertainties around trust. Your reactions to past events and experiences are understandable.

The fact that you are working through this study means you are committed to growing, and I am so proud of you for doing that.

7. Let's end our time together by reminding ourselves of what the Bible says about our feelings and how God looks at us when we are in pain. Fill in the blanks of the verses that follow. (We used the NIV for this question.)

Psalm 34:18—The LORD is close to the _____ and saves those who are _____.

1 Peter 5:7—Cast all your _____ on him because he _____ for you.

Psalm 145:18—The LORD is _____ all who call on him, to all who call on him in truth.

Ezekiel 36:26—"I will give you a _____ and put a _____ in you; I will remove from you your heart of _____ and give you a heart of _____."

8. To finish your personal study time, write a prayer using some of the wording from the verses listed in question 7.

Today, we're going to explore chapter 3 of the *I Want to Trust You, but I Don't* book. If you haven't had a chance to read chapter 3 yet, please do so before answering the questions.

Have you ever experienced a friendship that fell apart bit by bit? It can be confusing to try to figure out what's actually happening. My friend Linda's experience wasn't unique. I have walked down a similar path with a friend who pulled away but didn't address the situation honestly and directly. It can deeply affect your heart and mind.

1. Have you ever experienced a friend's hurtful and maybe confusing behavior? Did you address them directly? If so, what was the response? What did you learn from that experience?

This is just another example of what can happen when we ignore red flags. Unaddressed red flags that keep happening become defining hardships that can break the relationship.

It's so important to point out here that red flags aren't a sign to end a relationship. Instead they are a warning that something needs to be discussed. And aren't we so thankful for warning signs? Their very purpose is to get us to pay attention and ultimately keep us safe.

Throughout the Bible, God has given us warnings to keep us safe—emotionally, spiritually, and physically. These warnings are because He cares for us. God is omniscient, meaning He is all-knowing. He knows the past, present, and future. So when God gives a warning, it's because He knows the potential harm.

2. Let's take a look at some warnings found in the Bible. For each Bible verse, write the warning God is giving us. Then, write an action you could take to respond in a right way.

VERSE	WARNING	RESPONSE
1 THESSALONIANS 4:11		
1 TIMOTHY 5:13		
1 JOHN 2:15–17		
PROVERBS 3:5–6		
MATTHEW 7:15–17		
PROVERBS 13:20		

(If you are enjoying this exercise, here are some additional verses to look up: Romans 16:17; James 1:14–16; John 3:20–21; Proverbs 12:22; Ephesians 4:29; Revelation 22:15; Colossians 3:8–10; Proverbs 14:21; Ephesians 4:26–27; 1 John 1:8–10; 2 Timothy 3:1–5; Proverbs 28:13; Psalms 19:13–14; 1 John 3:4; Proverbs 6:16–19; Luke 6:45; 1 John 1:6–7.)

It's amazing that in addition to Scripture, God has given us an internal "warning sign" in the form of discernment.

I'm so thankful God doesn't leave us alone to figure out when a red flag is a misunderstanding or something more significant. When we accept Jesus as our Savior, we receive the gift of the Holy Spirit. This was a promise given back in the Old Testament (Joel 2) and confirmed by Jesus.

> But very truly I tell you, it is for your good that I am going away. Unless I go away, the Advocate will not come to you; but if I go, I will send him to you.
>
> **JOHN 16:7**

Jesus shared this promise on His last night with His disciples, right before He was betrayed in the Garden of Gethsemane. The disciples were confused because Jesus revealed He would be leaving them. But Jesus reassured them that He would send someone to them. That was the Holy Spirit, who will lead us into truth (John 16:13).

3. In Greek, the name translated "Advocate" in the NIV is *parakletos*. Interestingly, our Bibles differ in how they translate this word. Look up John 6:7 in these different versions. Write a short description, in your own words, of how the Holy Spirit will work in your life based on the word used to describe Him. (You can find different Bible translations for free online on sites like Biblegateway.com or on the YouVersion Bible App.)

CSB: Counselor

NIV: Advocate

ESV: Helper

TLB: Comforter

Depending on your Bible translation, you might not find the word "discernment." But we understand what it means through different scriptures. Here's a working definition of discernment we can use: "The sound judgment which makes possible the distinguishing of good from evil, and the recognition of God's right ways for his people. It is necessary for the understanding of spiritual realities and, on a practical level, for right government and the avoidance of life's pitfalls." [4]

---

4 Martin H. Manser, *Dictionary of Bible Themes: The Accessible and Comprehensive Tool for Topical Studies,* (London: Martin Manser, 2009).

4. The Bible gives us different examples of how discernment is used. Look up each verse and identify the purpose of discernment.

Philippians 1:9–10

2 Samuel 14:17

Proverbs 28:11

Hebrews 5:14

I've experienced discernment in many ways, but most of the time it's a gut feeling or a deep knowing. Please read the book excerpt below and answer the question that follows.

> "I like to think of discernment as the intimate way God cares for me, leads me, redirects me, warns me, and reveals things to me that I otherwise may miss on my own." (p. 36)

5. Have you ever experienced the feeling that God is guiding you? It might be as simple as a nudge or as clear as hearing His voice in your spirit. Write a few sentences about your experience to acknowledge and remind yourself that God can and does speak to you.

Reread Hebrews 5:14. What is the solid food mentioned here? What are the constant practices that help train our discernment?

As I shared in the book, sometimes my brain and heart come into conflict. When that happens, my discernment can feel off. That's when I need to use wisdom to avoid extremes. James 1:5 reads, *If any of you lacks wisdom, you should ask God, who gives generously to all without finding fault, and it will be given to you.*

So, not only does the Holy Spirit guide us, but God also gives us wisdom. Both discernment and wisdom can be cultivated through time spent in God's presence and in reading His Word. The combination of wisdom and discernment can help when we get off balance and our desires for safety and connection conflict. This is when it's important to have our minds renewed.

6. Why would we need to renew our minds in order to experience clearer and wiser discernment and wisdom?

7. Sometimes, we long so deeply for a connection with someone that we are willing to overlook concerning behaviors and red flags. At other times, if our highest priority is safety, we might miss out on relationships because we want very little risk.

Where on this priority spectrum do you fall?

I MUST HAVE
HIGH CONNECTION ├────────────────────────────────┤ I MUST HAVE
HIGH SAFETY

Write any thoughts you have about this.

8. Our goal is to bring these back into balance with authentic connections that have depth, but we are paying attention to safety. What might you need to change in a current relationship to bring it back in balance?

It can get confusing for a Christian to know how to love someone who is breaking trust. But the Bible doesn't tell us to *trust* unconditionally—just *love* unconditionally. Jesus told His disciples to: *"Love one another. As I have loved you, so you must love one another"* (John 13:34).

Please read the book excerpt below and answer the questions that follow.

> "... instead of shooting for unconditional trust where we are blind to red flags and expected to overlook them, we need to shift from blind trust to wise trust." (p. 38)

9. What are some of the dangers of blind trust? To ourselves and to our relationships? Feel free to refer back to chapter 3 in the book for your answers or provide your own insight here.

10. What does wise trust require?

As we wrap up our time this week, I invite you to review the eleven red flags one more time. We've talked about red flags in our video discussion and previously in your personal time. I went into greater detail in this chapter and included more examples of what each red flag looks like. My hope is you feel better equipped to process and discern what is eroding trust in your relationships.

11. As you read through them, did you have any new insights or revelations, either about yourself or a relationship? Write them here.

DAYS 4 & 5

Read chapters 4 and 5.

Use these days to go back and complete any of the reflection questions or activities from the previous days this week that you weren't able to finish. Make note of any revelations you've had and reflect on any growth or personal insights you've gained.

Spend the next two days reading chapters 4 and 5 in the *I Want to Trust You, but I Don't* book. Use the space below to note anything in the chapters that stands out to you or encourages your heart.

Schedule

BEFORE YOUR GROUP GATHERING	Read chapters 4–5 in the *I Want to Trust You, but I Don't* book.
GROUP GATHERING	Watch Video Session 3 Group Discussion Pages 72–82
PERSONAL STUDY DAY 1	Study guide pages 83–89
PERSONAL STUDY DAY 2	Study guide pages 90–95
PERSONAL STUDY DAY 3	Study guide pages 96–101
PERSONAL STUDY DAYS 4 & 5	Read chapters 6–7 in the *I Want to Trust You, but I Don't* book.

Session 3

Trust Is a Track Record

WELCOME AND OPENING REFLECTION:
(Suggested time: 15–20 minutes)

Welcome to Session 3 of *I Want to Trust You, but I Don't.*

Leader Note: Before starting the video, take a few moments to check in with your group about how they are doing. Let the group warm up a bit by asking if there was anything from their personal study time they'd like to share with the group.

Another option is to ask this question:

What was a helpful takeaway from chapters 4 and 5 of the book?

VIDEO:
(Run time: 15 minutes)

Leader Note: Play the teaching video for Session 3.

As you watch the video, use the outline below to help you follow along with the teaching and take additional notes on anything that stands out to you.

Kintsugi—the Japanese art of repair.

Every break or rip is unique. So, every repair needs to be unique. More severe breaks will require more time for the repair.

God modeled the principle of repairing rips in relationships throughout Scripture and implements it in our relationship with Him and others.

The most severe rip in a relationship is between God and man in Genesis 3 when the first sin occurred.

God won't do anything that is inconsistent with His nature and character because then He would cease to be God. This means God will not have any part in sin.

In the Old Testament, as sin increased, the presence of God decreased.

Then the man and his wife heard the sound of the LORD God as he was walking in the garden in the cool of the day, and they hid from the LORD God among the trees of the garden. But the LORD God called to the man, "Where are you?" (Genesis 3:8–9)

So the LORD God banished him from the Garden of Eden to work the ground from which he had been taken. (Genesis 3:23)

Then the LORD said to Cain, "Why are you angry? Why is your face downcast? If you do what is right, will you not be accepted? But if you do not do what is right, sin is crouching at your door; it desires to have you, but you must rule over it." (Genesis 4:6–7)

The LORD saw how great the wickedness of the human race had become on the earth, and that every inclination of the thoughts of the human heart was only evil all the time. (Genesis 6:5)

God always puts into place ways for His people to stay connected to Him.

Despite the increased presence of sin, God always provided a connection point back to Himself.

Altars (see Genesis 8:20)

The Tabernacle (see Exodus 25:8–9)

The Ark of the Covenant (see Exodus 37)

The Temple (see 1 Kings 6:1, 37–38)

Jesus (see Matthew 1:18–25)

God's trustworthiness is a track record for us to cling to.

Repentance must be present in order for the repair process to work in human relationships.

Repentance happens when sin is addressed and the individual agrees to turn from that sin.

Where sin goes unaddressed and people aren't cooperative with the repair process, reconciliation will become increasingly challenging.

Ask yourself:

- Is this person being humble or prideful?
- Are they repentant and owning their actions, or are they stubborn and refusing to acknowledge their wrongdoing?
- Do they care about how their actions affected you?
- Do they seek forgiveness?
- Do they have a spirit of care and compassion toward you?

To the extent that trust is broken is the extent that it needs to be repaired.

The secret weapon of emotionally connected couples is the strength of the friendship and the emotional climate between partners.[5]

The daily deposits we make in our relationship really matter. Being a consistent positive, helpful, and kind presence in someone's life helps build a trust track record.

To protect that trust track record, it is wise to identify the daily ways micro rips happen in a relationship so we can repair those and stay fully present with one another.

---

5 See Kyle Benson, "Repair Is the Secret of Emotionally Connected Couples," Gottman Institute, www.gottman.com/blog/repair–secret–weapon–emotionally–connected–couples, accessed May 22, 2024.

The 5-Step Framework for a Repair Conversation:

- First, what am I feeling . . .
- Then, what is feeding the feeling . . .
- Now, what are the facts . . .
- Once we know the facts, let's figure out what we both need . . .
- And lastly, let's find a way forward . . .

Group Discussion

(SUGGESTED TIME 40–45 MINUTES)

Leader Note: We have included some questions to get your group discussion started. Feel free to add your own or modify what's here. The goal is for your group to have a meaningful discussion.

1. The Session 3 video featured an example of *kintsugi,* the process of repairing a broken piece of pottery by using gold to fill in the broken spaces. How does that example help you understand how God redeems and remakes our lives?

2. If you have an example of how God turned something broken into something beautiful in your life, please share it with the group.

The Bible is God's recorded history of repairing the most severe broken relationship in history—between humankind and God. The story of the temptation and fall of Adam and Eve is told in Genesis 3. In Week 2, we looked back at Genesis to see how this decision affected the relationship between God and His creation. Now let's look at how God responded.

3. In the video, Lysa pointed out that as sin increased, the presence of God decreased. Have one member of your group read Genesis 3:17–24 aloud, then answer the following questions.

- What consequences does God pronounce on Adam and Eve in verses 17–19?

- In what ways do these consequences resonate with experiences in your life and in the world today?

- How would the banishment of Adam and Eve from Eden have affected their relationship with God? What would have changed?

- How do we see the kindness of God in these verses?

4. The Bible tells us that unfortunately, the consequences for Adam and Eve didn't lead to the repentance of God's people. We see this just a few chapters later in Genesis, where we read about Noah. Read Genesis 6:5–8 aloud.

   - From what we read in verse 5, what would life have been like on earth? What would have been missing from human interaction?

   - Despite God's judgment on humanity, we still see evidence of His grace and mercy. What evidence of that do you see in this passage?

- How does the story of Noah and the flood point to the ultimate reconciliation offered through Jesus?

5. Even though humankind started over with Noah, people continued to sin. Yet, despite the increased presence of sin, God always provided a connection point back to Himself. Lysa referenced five examples of how God showed His longing for His people.

Have someone read each passage aloud, and then as a group, identify the connection point.

PASSAGE	CONNECTION POINT
GENESIS 8:20–22	
EXODUS 25:8–9	
EXODUS 25:10–22 (FOR FURTHER DETAIL, READ EXODUS 37)	
1 KINGS 6:1, 37–38	
MATTHEW 1:18–25	

6. Share any observations you might have after reading about God's intentionality to be with us.

In the video, Lysa shared this statement:

> "The rip started with humanity, and so Jesus, who is fully God and fully man, entered human history in order to restore and repair that rip. Because of His sacrifice, we can enjoy the personal presence of God through the Holy Spirit today."

7. Why is God's intentionality to repair damaged relationships crucial to understand when talking about human-to-human relationships?

8. Why is this important when talking about our relationship with God?

9. Lysa shared a framework that helps her express her needs when there are trust breaches. Read through the five prompts. Then, as a group, identify a common situation in relationships, and apply the framework. Lysa's example is included to help give you some ideas.

FRAMEWORK	LYSA'S EXAMPLE	GROUP EXAMPLE
WHAT AM I FEELING?	Frustrated	
WHAT IS FEEDING THE FEELING?	Worried that spouse isn't organized enough with bills	
WHAT ARE THE FACTS?	Two late notices	
FIGURE OUT WHAT WE BOTH NEED.	A system both people agree to	
FIND A WAY FORWARD.	Do a check-in on the first of each month	

10. The overall message of the video is that trust is a track record. Close your meeting with members sharing how God has a proven track record of trust in their lives. Give practical examples of how God has been faithful.

CLOSING:
(Suggested time: 5 minutes)

Leader Note: Read the following instructions and clarify any questions your group may have about the homework and what each participant should do between now and the next session. Then, take a few minutes to pray with your group. You can use the prayer provided or pray your own prayer.

BEFORE THE NEXT SESSION . . .

Every week, the *I Want to Trust You, but I Don't Study Guide* includes five days of personal study to help you make meaningful connections between your life and what you're learning each week. This week, you'll do more review of the video we discussed today, and then work through chapters 4 and 5 of the *I Want to Trust You, but I Don't* book. You'll also have time to read chapters 6 and 7 of the book in preparation for our next study together.

PRAYER

Dear Lord, You are the Creator of the universe, the One who desires to be in an intimate relationship with Your creation. Your Word tells us that You delight in being with Your people, and that Your heart longs to dwell among us. Thank You for pursuing us with your perfect love. We are grateful for the gift of Your presence and the assurance that You will never leave us nor forsake us. Lord, You came to dwell among us, to be Immanuel, "God with us." May we never take Your presence for granted, O Lord. Help us to be more aware of You, to abide in Your love, and to walk in step with Your Spirit. In Jesus' name, Amen.

Personal Study

DAY 1 | TRUST IS A TRACK RECORD

Today we will spend more time reflecting on Session 3 in the video series for *I Want to Trust You, but I Don't*. If you haven't had a chance to watch that session, please take some time to do so before beginning today's personal study.

It's amazing to me how God's natural design for us is to heal. Healing is in His nature, and it is woven into God's design for this world. We see this in our physical bodies,s which are designed to naturally fight off infection, and in our hearts, which heal over time from things like grief.

But due to the realities of sin, we know sometimes bodies don't heal, and sometimes hearts don't heal on their own either. At least not from a human perspective.

Even the rips and tears in our relationships can make us feel ruined. And when something seems ruined, it's easier to just throw it out than spend the time and money to repair it. These days, it can be more expensive to repair something than to replace it.

The good news is our God still pursues the healing of what is torn apart, ripped, broken, and seemingly ruined.

I think that's part of why I love the *kintsugi* example so much. Some might say that the repaired version, with the gold veins running throughout, is even more beautiful than the original. The gold doesn't highlight the breaks; instead, it creates a pattern of beauty that wouldn't be there without them.

1. Consider an example in your own life. Has something broken, but once repaired, it is even more beautiful? This could be something like a piece of jewelry or art, or it could be a relationship. Describe what happened and why the results are so pleasing.

In the video, I stated that as sin increased in the Old Testament, God's presence decreased. But God always made a way for His people to stay connected to Him. There are many examples in Scripture of this, but today, let's spend more time studying five areas where God and humanity connected.

THE ALTAR

Read Genesis 8:20.

This is the first mention in the Bible of an altar, and it comes after Noah left the ark. The Hebrew word for altar, *miz·bēaḥ*, comes from the verb for "to slaughter" and means "slaughter place." An altar could have been any structure made of earth, stone, brick, wood, or metal. Its purpose was to offer a sacrifice to God.

But it also represented a place where the divine and human worlds touched. It was where humanity offered a sacrifice and God accepted it.

2. This is the first recorded act of Noah after the flood. Why do you think Noah's first action was to build an altar and offer sacrifices?

3. What does this act reveal about Noah's relationship with God? What does God's response reveal about His relationship with Noah?

4. The idea of sacrifice might seem unusual to us today, but when done with the right heart, it is an act of love. What would make a sacrifice a profession of love for God?

5. Read 1 Samuel 15:22. This verse gives us an idea of how a sacrifice might not be acceptable to God. What might diminish the gift of a sacrifice in God's eyes?

THE TABERNACLE

Read Exodus 25:8–9.

Many years after Noah built an altar . . . after the patriarchs Abraham, Isaac, and Jacob lived . . . the Bible tells the story of Moses and how God freed His people from slavery in Egypt. Once the people were free and were journeying in the wilderness, God told His people to build a tabernacle.

6. Why did God want a tabernacle built?

7. What does this passage reveal about God's character and His desire to be near His people?

The Hebrew word for tabernacle is *mishkan,* which means "dwelling place" or "tent." This word is primarily used in the Old Testament, but we find an important usage of "dwelling" in the New Testament referring to Jesus.

> The Word became flesh and made his dwelling among us.
> We have seen his glory, the glory of the one and only Son,
> who came from the Father, full of grace and truth.
>
> **JOHN 1:14**

8. In light of God's desire to repair the rip in our relationship with Him, compare the two experiences of God coming to dwell among us: first, in the Old Testament tabernacle, and then, in Jesus' dwelling on earth. What similarities do you see? What differences do you see?

THE ARK OF THE COVENANT (SEE EXODUS 37)

Read Exodus 25:10–22.

The Ark of the Covenant was a sacred object described in the Bible as a wooden chest covered in gold with two cherubim on its lid, forming the "mercy seat." God gave specific instructions for its design and it served as a tangible symbol of God's presence. It was designed to be mobile and was kept in the inner sanctuary of the tabernacle and later in the temple in Jerusalem.

What is the purpose of the mercy seat, described in verses 17–22?

What does the term "mercy seat" tell us about God's character and His desire to connect with His people?

THE TEMPLE

Read 1 Kings 8:6–12.

After the Israelites had completed their wilderness wandering, King Solomon built the first temple to provide a place of worship for the people and to house the Ark of the Covenant, where God dwelled.

Describe what happened when the priest brought the ark into the inner sanctuary (vv. 6–8).

What was inside the ark? From what you know, why would these items be important to keep as part of God's dwelling place?

What happened when the priest withdrew from the Holy Place? (vv. 10–11)

Read Exodus 40:34–35 and describe what happened when the tabernacle was dedicated.

JESUS

The ultimate connection point between God and His people is Jesus. We could spend so much more time today studying Jesus and the incredible gift of His presence. But as we come close to the end of this day, let's focus on a few verses in the Gospel of John. Write John 1:1–5 in the space provided below, then respond to the question.

What do these verses reveal about Jesus' connection with God? With us?

Take a few moments to reflect on what this means to you that Jesus was with God and was God. Write any thoughts you have.

The five examples we just studied show God's track record of trustworthiness. The rip started with humanity, and Jesus entered our world to repair that rip and restore our relationship with God. Because of His sacrifice, we enjoy God's presence through the Holy Spirit today.

There's one more part of this process we should consider, and that's the importance of repentance.

Using the NIV Bible, fill in the blanks of the following verses:

Acts 3:19: "_____, then, and _____, so that your sins may be _____, that times of _____ may come from the Lord."

2 Corinthians 7:10a: Godly _____ brings _____ that leads to _____ and leaves no regret . . .

2 Corinthians 5:18–19: All this is from God, who _____ us to himself through _____ and gave us the ministry of reconciliation: that _____was _____ the world to himself in _____, not counting people's _____ against them.

The Bible shows us that sin must be addressed in order for the repair process to be effective, and that repentance must be part of reconciliation.

As we wrap up, in the video, I invited you to think about a rip that needs some repair work in one of your relationships. What part of today's teaching most applies to your situation? What did it help you see? What do you now need to do?

Today we are going to explore chapter 4 in the *I Want to Trust You, but I Don't* book. If you haven't already read chapter 4, please do so before you begin.

A significant truth to remember as we work through this idea of broken trust is that our hearts weren't designed to be deeply wounded by painful and fractured relationships. We were made for unity—with God and with others. We have seen this in our study of Genesis where God, Adam, and Eve were in a perfect relationship. But then we also saw how sin causes separation.

We already studied yesterday how God provides ways to stay connected with His people and bridge the gap between a holy God and imperfect people. Today, let's look at how broken trust in human-to-human relationships complicates and compromises the place where we should be our most authentic selves.

It's in our human relationships that we are to love and be loved as God designed. But sin creates the disconnections, dysfunctions, and sometimes devastations to God's original plan for loving relationships.

As we are learning, trust is truly the foundation of every relationship. It's not always something we can define, but we definitely know when it's not there.

1. Based on what you've learned so far and your own personal experience, write your definition of trust:

2. In order to build trust, we must decide what we need in order to consider the other person trustworthy. Interestingly, this differs from person to person. Having an idea of what's important to you will help you start to put words to your feelings when trust is broken.

Take some time to review this list and check the five that are most important to you.

- ☐ They are who they say they are
- ☐ They do what they say they are going to do
- ☐ They show up with care and compassion
- ☐ They tell the truth
- ☐ They use good judgment and biblical wisdom in their decisions
- ☐ They aren't moody, unpredictable, or prone to angry outbursts
- ☐ You can count on them to be there for you
- ☐ They have longevity in their other relationships
- ☐ They are humble enough to admit they are sometimes wrong
- ☐ They are willing to be held accountable
- ☐ They don't dance around issues but instead are straightforward
- ☐ They don't cut corners or cheat
- ☐ They respect other people's property
- ☐ They respect your time

3. There are levels of severity with broken trust. There are rips and there are full-blown ruptures. It's probably fair to assume that you've chosen to read this book because you have experienced your share of rips and ruptures. But maybe you've never considered there's a range of severity. In this next exercise, you'll have a chance to consider the areas of broken trust you've faced or are currently facing.

With each experience, you'll identify three things:

1. The relationship (you can identify this however you want, with a name, initials, or some other way that allows you to be discreet)
2. What's lacking that is causing the broken trust? (the list from chapter 4 is included on the following page for your convenience)
3. Finally, using the spectrum, identify where that relationship is.

Examples of what's lacking:

- integrity

- competence

- reliability

- care and compassion

- good judgment

- humility

- stability

NAME _____

WHAT'S LACKING _____

RIP | | | | | | | | | RUPTURE

NAME _____

WHAT'S LACKING _____

RIP | | | | | | | | | RUPTURE

NAME _____

WHAT'S LACKING _____

RIP | | | | | | | | | RUPTURE

4. For those issues that are rips, what are some things you can do to address them before they become ruptures?

Getting to the root issue of the problem can help repair the rips in relationships. There's a surface reason our trust starts to erode (a series of forgotten meetings), but then there could be a root problem (potentially a lack of care or maybe low reliability). God is so good at getting to the heart of an issue, and we can learn some things from Him.

The prophet Samuel was assigned the task of finding the king who would replace Saul, Israel's first king. God knew the future King David was a son of Jesse. When Samuel reviewed the most obvious choices, God taught Samuel (and us) a lesson about what's important to Him.

5. What does the following verse tell us about what's important to God?

> But the Lord said to Samuel, "Do not consider his appearance or his height, for I have rejected him. The Lord does not look at the things people look at. People look at the outward appearance, but the Lord looks at the heart."
>
> **1 SAMUEL 16:7**

God is consistent in looking at our hearts. We might be able to look good on the outside, but if our insides don't match our outsides, roots will start to grow and problems will eventually arise. The more we tend to what's inside our hearts, the better we will be at seeing it in others.

6. I've shared that the series of broken trust scenarios I walked through changed me. Rather than being a noticer of good, my eyes tended to look for what was wrong or out of place. However, I've learned it's possible to have a healthy balance between using wise discernment and seeing evidence of God's work in a person's life.

When suspicion looms large, it can feel unsafe to trust actions, even if they look good. But though we can't see a person's heart, we can see if their actions are in alignment with the fruit of the Spirit, which is evidence of God's Spirit working in them.

The apostle Paul provides a list of good things we can cultivate in our hearts and look for in others. When we see fruit grow, we can trust that a root of goodness is growing as well.

For each fruit mentioned in Galatians 5:22–25, write some actions that we should see demonstrated in a person's life. We used the CSB translation for this exercise:

> But the fruit of the Spirit is love, joy, peace, patience, kindness, goodness, faithfulness, gentleness, and self-control. The law is not against such things. Now those who belong to Christ Jesus have crucified the flesh with its passions and desires. If we live by the Spirit, let us also keep in step with the Spirit.

FRUIT OF THE SPIRIT	WHAT MIGHT YOU SEE IF A PERSON IS NOT DEMONSTRATING THIS FRUIT OF THE SPIRIT?	WHAT SHOULD BE DEMONSTRATED IN A PERSON'S LIFE WITH THIS FRUIT OF THE SPIRIT?
LOVE		
JOY		
PEACE		
PATIENCE		
KINDNESS		
GOODNESS		
FAITHFULNESS		
GENTLENESS		
SELF-CONTROL		

To wrap up our time together today, consider this quote from the book:

> "The ties that bind us are incredibly strong until they are made fragile because of choices that sliced away at what should have been protected."
> (p. 60)

Though we can't change what other people do, we can always look at our own choices. In every relationship, we have a chance to strengthen the bond. Based on what you've learned so far in our time together, identify two or three of your closest relationships, and write down a choice you can make this week to strengthen the ties that bind you in the space allotted below.

RELATIONSHIP   MY CHOICE

_____   _____

_____   _____

_____   _____

Friend, we've processed a lot so far in this study. If you feel overwhelmed today by anything, or if sadness is weighing heavy on your heart, I want to share this prayer, from chapter 4, that helps me on really hard days:

Lord, help me to see what I need to see. Hear what I need to hear. Know what I need to know. And do what I need to do. In Jesus' name, Amen.

Today we are going to explore chapter 5 in the *I Want to Trust You, but I Don't* book. If you haven't already read chapter 5, please do so before you begin.

I started this chapter by sharing my experience of feeling alone. Loneliness doesn't always mean you are physically alone. You can be surrounded by people you love and trust, but if you are carrying the burden of something heavy with no one to process it with, you can feel very alone.

Today as we start our study together, it's okay for you to pause and express an area where you feel alone. You may have a close relationship with someone you trust, but maybe you don't feel quite safe sharing every thought. Or perhaps you've been carrying some concerns or suspicions but don't feel ready to say anything. I know what that feels like, and it's scary.

One of my goals in writing this book and corresponding study guide is to somehow reach through the pages so you feel less alone. I pray this study can be a place for you to process some of those thoughts and feelings through the words of Scripture.

Let's start today by reminding ourselves that we have a God who helps us carry burdens that feel too heavy. We also have a God who invites us to share those thoughts that are hard to put into words. The Bible even says when we don't have the words, the Holy Spirit helps us pray in groans (see Romans 8:26).

1. Write down a burden, concern, or worry that you are carrying alone. If that seems too hard, just write a word or name.

2. When we have our trust broken, it's tempting to replace trust with control. If we can stay in control of situations, then we falsely believe we can avoid the risks of trust. But when we try to control a person or situation, we are seeking our will over God's will. Read Proverbs 3:5–6. Write these verses in your own words.

3. What happens when we try to live life avoiding risk? Write down a situation where you've found yourself avoiding an opportunity because of the risk.

I shared a bit about being a guest on a podcast when the interviewer shifted the conversation from receiving advice to giving advice. I'd just confidently declared that dating wasn't for me when she suggested that perhaps it wasn't too late for me.

For me, in that situation, "never too late" applied to whether I would date. But the "never too late" idea is so profound because it's rooted in the reality that we serve a God who can do anything at any time. He never writes us off as too far gone, or too far away from Him, or too old or too young. Really, we are never "too" anything for God.

4. It's interesting that some of the heroes of our faith felt the same way. They thought it was too late for them, or maybe others thought that about them. But God didn't. God still had a good future planned for them, just as He has a good future planned for you.

Let's spend a few minutes reminding ourselves of a few of these stories. Read the summary and question. Then read the Bible verse to identify what God did in the lives of these "Never Too Late" people.

ABRAHAM   GENESIS 21:1–2

Abraham was a hundred years old and his wife Sarah was ninety. What promise did God fulfill in their lives?

MOSES   EXODUS 3:10–12

Moses was older and considered himself slow of speech. How did God use Him?

PAUL   1 CORINTHIANS 15:9–10

The apostle Paul was a Jew who persecuted Christians. He was the least likely person to become a follower of Jesus. How did God use Paul?

Maybe right now, your good future is hard to envision. You feel locked in the pain and the past. Or you feel stuck in the present. Maybe your trust in yourself is shaken by what you've missed or allowed. If big leaps forward feel too risky right now, is there a baby step you can take?

5. My baby step was to be much more cautious of using the word "never." Write one baby step you can take that will help create some forward momentum toward your healing.

The rhythm of moving forward will feel more empowering than you think possible. Instead of waiting for things to happen to me, moving forward allowed things to happen while I made progress in my own life.

Isaiah 30:19–21 has been such a comfort for me as I take these baby steps toward trust. I've provided some historical context for this verse and then some questions to consider.

> 19) *People of Zion, who live in Jerusalem, you will weep no more. How gracious he will be when you cry for help! As soon as he hears, he will answer you.*
> 20) *Although the Lord gives you the bread of adversity and the water of affliction, your teachers will be hidden no more; with your own eyes you will see them.*
> 21) *Whether you turn to the right or to the left, your ears will hear a voice behind you, saying, "This is the way; walk in it."*

This prophecy from Isaiah came at a time when the people of Judah were trying to create an alliance with Egypt to fight the Assyrians. But this wasn't God's plan, and the entire nation of Judah was walking in disobedience. So God sent Isaiah to warn them of their sin of choosing their own way.

6. Chapter 30 starts off with these words from God: "Woe to the obstinate children." How does knowing verse 19 was written to people whom God considered stubbornly disobedient give you encouragement when you are walking out of alignment with God's best for you?

7. The Israelites were looking to Egypt for help, rather than looking to God. Read verse 19 again and underline what God will do when we cry for help.

In verse 20, Isaiah refers to "teachers" who have been hidden. Translators differ in their interpretation of whether the original Hebrew word for teacher—*moreka*— was singular or plural.

The NIV translators (the version used primarily in this study) believe it was plural and likely referred to the prophets and priests of God who had been teaching God's Word.[6]

However, the Christian Standard Bible translates *moreka* as singular, as shown in verse 20: *The Lord will give you meager bread and water during oppression, but your Teacher will not hide any longer. Your eyes will see your Teacher.*

This translation suggests the Teacher is God Himself and that He will reveal Himself over time. In the New Testament we see the Teacher revealed as first Jesus and then the Holy Spirit (Matthew 23:10, Luke 12:12).[7]

Whether it's "teacher" or "teachers," God is saying there is danger when we reject godly wisdom and turn to our own ways. The more we choose our will, the less sensitive we are to God's voice, eventually not hearing Him at all.

8. Can you look back to a time in your life when you might have turned from some godly wisdom and turned to yourself or other voices? How did that impact where you are today?

Now, let's look at verse 21, which gives me great hope. When we desire to be led by God's Spirit, we can trust that even if we make wrong choices, God will not abandon us. It's not like there's a perfect path, and we'll miss it if we turn left or right, but it's a process of seeking God's redirection to His will and trusting that He will provide it.

---

6 J. Alec Motyer, *Isaiah: An Introduction and Commentary,* Vol. 20, Tyndale Old Testament Commentaries, (Downers Grove, IL: InterVarsity Press, 1999), 20:223.

7 *The CSB Study Bible for Women* (Nashville: Holman Bible Publishers, 2018), note on Isaiah 30:20 (p. 875).

9. Based on Isaiah 30:19–21, what can you do to increase your awareness of God's presence and desire to lead you with His wisdom?

To close our time together, think about these words: Whenever we are waiting *on God*, we are actually waiting *with God*. Spend some time in prayer thanking God for His nearness to you. Confess your desire to go your own way and recommit to listening for His voice.

DAYS 4 & 5

Read chapters 6 and 7.

Use these days to go back and complete any of the reflection questions or activities from the previous days this week that you weren't able to finish. Make note of any revelations you've had and reflect on any growth or personal insights you've gained.

Spend the next two days reading chapters 6 and 7 of the *I Want to Trust You, but I Don't* book. Use the space below to note anything in the chapters that stands out to you or encourages your heart.

Schedule

BEFORE YOUR GROUP GATHERING	Read chapters 6–7 in the *I Want to Trust You, but I Don't* book.
GROUP GATHERING	Watch Video Session 4 Group Discussion Pages 104–113
PERSONAL STUDY DAY 1	Study guide pages 114–119
PERSONAL STUDY DAY 2	Study guide pages 120–125
PERSONAL STUDY DAY 3	Study guide pages 126–132
PERSONAL STUDY DAYS 4 & 5	Read chapters 8–9 in the *I Want to Trust You, but I Don't* book.

The More I Doubt Him, the Less I'll Trust Him

WELCOME AND OPENING REFLECTION:
(Suggested time: 15–20 minutes)

Welcome to Session 4 of *I Want to Trust You, but I Don't.*

Leader Note: Before starting the video, take a few moments to check in with your group about how they are doing. Let the group warm up a bit by asking if there was anything from their personal study time they'd like to share with the group.

Another option is to ask this question:

What was a helpful takeaway from chapters 6 and 7 of the book?

VIDEO:
(Run time: 20 minutes)

Leader Note: Play the teaching video for Session 4.

As you watch the video, use the outline below to help you follow along with the teaching and take additional notes on anything that stands out to you.

"What is true about the heart of God?"

What we believe about God's true nature will affect how we process the really hard things that happen in life.

For my friend Lisa, trusting God was never about what she was facing in the moment . . . but rather about confidence in the consistent faithfulness He displayed throughout her life.

> Brothers and sisters, we do not want you to be uninformed about those who sleep in death, so that you do not grieve like the rest of mankind, who have no hope. For we believe that Jesus died and rose again, and so we believe that God will bring with Jesus those who have fallen asleep in him.
>
> **1 THESSALONIANS 4:13–14**

Being open to the joys of life even in the midst of hardships feels like a beautiful definition of hope.

If we believe that God loves us so much that He would give His only Son to die for us, why would we think that His love would stop on the threshold of devastating life circumstances and things that don't make sense to us?

The more I trust the absolute love God has for me . . . the more I can trust Him.

If we believe that the Lord is cruel, it will shape what we do and how we think. And if we think He's not trustworthy, then we will never act like He's trustworthy.

If I believe that God allows harsh realities for no good reason, I will want to try to control my circumstances rather than trust His plan.

What I don't trust I will try to control.

The Parable of the Talents is found in Matthew 25:14–30.

The action of the servant who hid the talent in the ground was a reflection of what he believed about the master.

Some historical facts about this parable:

- A talent was a measure of weight (50–75 pounds) with a monetary value of 6,000 silver denarii

- Wealthy people regularly went on long journeys

- Wealthy landowners could lend money

- The practice of burying money was common

Burying the talent over investing it was the servant putting his agenda before the master's.

The third servant didn't want to risk a bad investment, but he didn't do what was asked of him, which is the definition of disobedience.

This disobedience reveals a lack of trust that the master knew best.

The word often translated "lazy" (*oknēros*) means "fearful."

The way the master wanted his investments to grow was through the obedience of the servants.

He wanted obedience more than he wanted the guarantee of making more money.

Sometimes we would rather be in control than be fully obedient. Especially if that obedience seems risky.

It's more important for us to be obedient to God and do what He asks us to do than to try to figure out things on our own.

Whatever uncontrollable thing comes your way, God is still in control.

Group Discussion

(SUGGESTED TIME 40–45 MINUTES)

Leader Note: We have included some questions to get your group discussion started. Feel free to add your own or modify what's here. The goal is for your group to have a meaningful discussion on the topics presented in this session's video.

1. In the video, Lysa shared a story about a godly woman who trusted God deeply. Share one thing from this story that inspired you or touched your heart.

2. In wrestling through the loss of her friend, Lysa asked herself an important question: What is true about the heart of God? The answer to this question can determine how we filter all of our experiences in this world. Let's look at some verses that show us God's true nature.

   Have someone read each verse. Then, as a group, identify what we can learn about God's character from His Word. Feel free to include as much as you can from each verse.

VERSE	GOD'S CHARACTER
NUMBERS 23:19	
PSALM 18:30	
PSALM 116:5–9	
JAMES 1:17	
1 JOHN 4:9	
TITUS 3:4–5	

If you enjoyed this exercise, here are more verses for you to research and identify elements of God's character: Matthew 6:26; Deuteronomy 20:3–4; Psalm 119:76; Psalm 147:4–5; Ephesians 3:20.

3. The more we trust God's love for *us,* the more we can trust *Him.* The challenge we have as humans is that we can have a different opinion about what love looks like. To understand how God loves us, we need to go to His Word. Romans 8 contains some clear expressions of God's love.

Read the verses below and discuss them as a group. What do they say about God's love for us? And what does this mean for us?

Romans 8:16–17

Romans 8:28–30

Romans 8:3–32

Romans 8:37–39

4. In the video, Lysa shared this idea:

> "If I believe that God allows harsh realities for no good reason, I will want to try and control my circumstances rather than trust His plan. What I don't trust I will try to control."

Share some common areas of life where it can be easier to try and control the outcome rather than trust in God's timing.

In last week's study, we looked at how we can know someone's heart based on the fruit they demonstrate in their lives. In the Parable of the Talents, Jesus affirmed the importance of external activity being evidence of internal faithfulness. It's not what we say, it's what we do that matters when it comes to building trust with others.

Have someone in your group read the parable of the talents aloud. It's found in Matthew 25:14–30. We recommend the CSB or NIV translations.

5. Verse 15 says that each man was entrusted with a different amount of gold according to his ability. Obviously, the master saw something different in each of his servants and entrusted them with a different amount. In light of our conversation about trusting and obeying, how might the servants have demonstrated their trustworthiness in the past?

6. Even though the first two servants earned different amounts of money, the master's response was the same. What did the future look like for the first two servants because of their obedience?

7. In verses 24 and 25, what excuse did the third servant give for not investing the money? What might it mean to harvest where someone hasn't sown? What do these verses tell us about how the servant viewed the master?

It's important to note that the master's goal in entrusting his servants with gold wasn't to keep his investment safe; it was growth. And we also learn that God's assignments to us can include risk. Investing the gold was risky, but it was also obedience. Read the quote from the video and answer the following questions.

> "It's more important for us to be obedient to God and do what He has asked us to do than to try to figure out things on our own."

8. If you are fiercely independent, the idea of "obedience" to any person might ruffle some of your feathers. Or maybe you think that only children need to obey. But throughout Scripture, God calls His children to obey Him. And when we trust someone, we are more likely to do what they ask.

   Why is trust so important to obedience? What happens when there is a lack of trust in the person who gives you a direction?

9. Wrap up your time together by reading the following passages about how we can let God's Word lead our thoughts and not the other way around. What are some action steps we can take this week based on each of these verses?

   2 Corinthians 10:5
   Philippians 4:8
   Psalm 119:11
   Ephesians 4:20–24

CLOSING:

(Suggested time: 5 minutes)

Leader Note: Read the following instructions and clarify any questions your group may have about the homework and what each participant should do between now and the next session. Then take a few minutes to pray with your group. You can use the prayer provided or pray your own prayer.

BEFORE THE NEXT SESSION . . .

Every week, the *I Want to Trust You, but I Don't Study Guide* includes five days of personal study to help you make meaningful connections between your life and what you're learning each week. This week, you'll do more review of the video we discussed today, and then work through chapters 6 and 7 of the *I Want to Trust You, but I Don't* book. You'll also have time to read chapters 8 and 9 of the book in preparation for our next study together.

PRAYER

Dear Lord, in the midst of our unpredictable and uncertain lives, we acknowledge that You are the only One we can fully trust. We confess that many times we have tried to control our lives rather than submit to You. Help us in the areas where we lack trust so that we can walk confidently in times of doubt and fear, knowing You have been faithful in the past and You will be faithful now. We want to obey You fully, knowing You are a good God. Thank You for your unfailing love. In Jesus' name, Amen.

Personal Study

Today we're going to spend a little more time reflecting on Session 4 of the video series. If you haven't had a chance to watch it, please do so before working through today's study.

In the video, I shared a very personal story about a deep loss I experienced. It's interesting how easy it is to take our faith in God for granted when life is predictable and comfortable. It's not until we're tested with something completely unexpected that we question why God didn't prevent this. Or we might wonder if God is even there.

Maybe you've said something like this before:

How can a good God let _____ happen?

Life is filled with loss. Sometimes the loss is because someone we love passed away. Other times, it's because someone we thought we could trust walked away. And the resulting grief from these types of losses hurts so deeply.

1. Let's start today's study with an honest assessment of some of our deep questions about God. Write down some of the questions that have been weighing on your heart. If this feels uncomfortable, remember that honesty is an important part of trust, and God can handle your honesty.

2. As I have walked through deep pain, I have found that asking God hard, honest questions has opened my heart to receive understanding. I don't always get clear answers, but I know I can find reassurance of God's love for me in His Word. The more I trust the absolute love God has for me . . . the more I can trust Him.

   Write the following verses and circle any words that stand out to you in each of them.

   Zephaniah 3:17

   Psalm 149:4

   Ephesians 3:17–19

   1 John 3:1

3. What we believe to be true about God is so important! It will truly define everything in our lives, starting with how we see ourselves and then filtering through all of our life experiences in this world. Let's start with some very general ideas about God and how these beliefs can shape our thoughts, beliefs, and actions.

IF I BELIEVE THIS . . .	THEN I WILL THINK, BELIEVE, OR ACT LIKE THIS . . .
GOD IS GOOD.	
GOD IS GOOD TO ME.	
GOD IS GOOD AT BEING GOD.	

4. Now let's look at what the Bible says about the character of God. Remember, God's unchanging character is His personal promise to us. If you are working through this study with a group, then you have already looked at some verses showing us God's character. Let's look at some more. As you read each verse, fill in the corresponding blank that shows a character trait of God.

VERSE	GOD IS
GENESIS 22:14	
ROMANS 2:4	
MALACHI 3:6	
1 JOHN 1:5	
1 JOHN 4:8	
2 PETER 3:9	
EXODUS 34:5–7	

5. It's one thing to write out all of God's wonderful characteristics, but it's quite another to believe them. It's like when we believe God answers other people's prayers, but maybe not ours. I've found if I want my experiences in life to change, then I need to address what I believe about God.

In question 3, we answered some general questions about how our beliefs about God change us. But now, let's get very personal. How has what you believe to be true about God shaped you in the following ways?

What you think about yourself:

What you believe about your purpose in life:

How you process the painful things that happen to you:

What you believe about your future:

Whether or not you trust God:

6. In the video, I shared that if I believe God allows harsh realities for no good reason, I will want to try to control my circumstances rather than trust His plan. What I don't trust I will try to control. For example, if we don't trust that God is working in the lives of our children, we will try to keep them from experiencing negative consequences. Or if we don't trust that God will bring the right spouse into our lives soon enough, we might make some unwise choices.

How have you experienced this in your own life? Write some examples of areas where you've tried to control rather than trust.

Sometimes, we would rather be in control than fully obedient, especially if that obedience seems risky. Let's spend more time looking at the parable Jesus told about the three servants and the man who entrusted them with his money. We see an example of obedience that seems risky and learn what can happen when we let fear lead our decisions.

Read Matthew 25:14–30.

7. Why did the master give differing amounts of talents (gold) to the different servants? What does this already tell us about the three men?

8. In this parable we see evidence of trust going both ways: first, the master to the servants, and second, the servants to the master. We are in many similar situations where this kind of two-way trust is seen. This can be in a work situation or in any group where there is a leader. Can you think of a situation where the trust of someone in authority (parent, teacher, boss, leader) emboldened you to try something that on your own you never would have done?

9. How did you feel about *their* trust in you? In reverse, how did *your* trust in them make a difference?

Stepping out in faith is risky at times. But as we've learned today, we serve a God who is faithful, kind, and merciful. He is a God of second chances . . . and many more.

10. To move from a place of reluctance into obedience, what is one thing you can do this week to grow in an area that God has called you to grow?

To wrap up today, spend time in prayer, asking God to help you trust Him more fully and to reveal any areas where fear or mistrust may be hindering your obedience.

Today we are going to work through some of the concepts found in chapter 6 in the *I Want to Trust You, but I Don't* book. If you haven't already read chapter 6, please do so before you begin.

Have you ever looked at a messed-up situation and thought something like this: *Things would have gone better if I'd been in charge*? Or you might observe other people acting badly and think: *I would NEVER . . . !!*

It's dangerous to make assumptions because, given the right circumstances and pressures, we all have the potential to surprise ourselves with what we'd say or do. *But for the grace of God, there go I!*

Nevertheless, when people hurt me, my mind starts to think about how I would have handled things differently. As I shared in the opening of the chapter, I found my *I-would-never* thoughts easily shifted to my thoughts about God. Especially in the hardest parts of my story.

After processing this trend of my thoughts, I realized my trust in God was firmly attached to my desire for things to turn out as I thought they should. Can you relate to this idea?

1. What do you desire or expect God to do in your life right now that would confirm in your mind that He is good?

I wrestled with trusting God with what I could not see or know. I struggled with my own thoughts and doubted God would answer my prayers. Read this quote from the book and see if you've ever felt this way too.

> "God is good. I know this. But when the pain and suffering gets intense, I sometimes feel less and less certain that His goodness will come through for me." (p. 96)

2. Write down an area in your life where you, too, are wondering if God will come through for you.

There is no shame in admitting our doubts. It's a place of honesty. And it's understandable to wonder about God's intentions. The Bible is full of stories of God's faithful people who got frustrated waiting for God to act and then made a wrong choice.

3. That must be why God repeatedly reminds us not to trust our own wisdom but to look to Him in times of trouble. One place we find this encouragement is in the book of Proverbs. Proverbs aren't promises, but they are part of the wisdom literature with godly advice on how to live in a way that honors God and other humans.

   In Proverbs 3, we find the recorded words of King Solomon to his son about how to live wisely. As you read verses 5 and 6 below, use the space to the right of the verses to draw images, words, or pictures that come to mind.

   Trust in the LORD with all your heart

   and lean not on your own understanding;

   in all your ways submit to him,

   and he will make your paths straight.

4. The Hebrew word for heart *(leb)* encompasses more than our emotions. It can also incorporate our thinking and our will. So when we are asked to trust God with our hearts, it's an all-encompassing request that can feel pretty big. Consider the three areas below and identify what it might look like to lean on your own understanding compared to trusting in the Lord.

	LEANING ON MY OWN UNDERSTANDING CAN LOOK LIKE . . .	TRUSTING IN GOD CAN LOOK LIKE . . .
MY EMOTIONS		
MY THINKING		
MY WILL		

Leaning on my own understanding comes naturally. When I get caught off guard with a problem, especially if it's turmoil in a relationship, I instantly want to fix it. I want the tension to go away. I want peace to return. I feel anxious, frustrated, and determined to solve the issues in the way I think is best.

But can I just admit how exhausting that is? Especially when I realize I can only do what's within my control. I can't control everything and everyone involved. Therefore, I have to have faith in God's ability to handle things that I cannot. He is fully capable and has a complete understanding of what's best. But this kind of faith can be really scary unless we are confident in God's goodness.

For the rest of our time together, let's work through some questions and verses that will help point us toward God's goodness instead of letting our doubt point us toward distrust.

I've put some of the questions I posed in the chapter here for you to work through. In this first section, write down each thought of distrust, so they don't stay all jumbled up inside you as a big bundle of fear and anxiety.

I fear trusting God with _____, because He allowed _____ to happen in my past.

I fear trusting God with _____, because if He doesn't come through for me in the way I want Him to, I will suffer _____.

I fear trusting God with _____, because I don't think God will really _____.

I fear trusting God with the suffering and heartbreak I'll go through if _____ happens, and I fear I won't ever _____.

EXPRESSING YOUR TRUE FEELINGS TO GOD IS A BEAUTIFUL ACT OF TRUSTING GOD!

Next, let's look at Scripture in a new way. For each verse, write something that helps you learn more about what God thinks about you and His intentions toward you.

- *I will instruct you and teach you in the way you should go; I will counsel you with my loving eye on you.* (Psalm 32:8)

- *"The LORD does not look at the things people look at. People look at the outward appearance, but the Lord looks at the heart." (1 Samuel 16:7)*

- *"Your Father knows what you need before you ask him." (Matthew 6:8)*

- *May the God of hope fill you with all joy and peace as you trust in him, so that you may overflow with hope by the power of the Holy Spirit. (Romans 15:13)*

- *"For My thoughts are not your thoughts, nor are your ways My ways," says the Lord. "For as the heavens are higher than the earth, so are My ways higher than your ways, and My thoughts than your thoughts." (Isaiah 55:8–9 NKJV)*

- *If our hearts condemn us, we know that God is greater than our hearts, and he knows everything. (1 John 3:20)*

In this section, let's use God's Word to help us stay certain of His goodness even when we suffer. Read the following verses and answer the prompt.

Suffering is also a way to _____ (see Romans 5:3)

Suffering is also a way to _____ (see Isaiah 43:2)

Suffering is also a way to _____ (see Psalm 27:13–14)

Suffering is also a way to _____ (see Job 5:11)

Suffering is also a way to _____ (see John 16:20)

Suffering is also a way to _____ (see 1 Peter 5:10)

As we finish today's study, take some time to look for tangible, small ways we see God's goodness. Think about this past week and how you experienced God using each of your five senses.

SENSE	EVIDENCE OF GOD'S GOODNESS
SIGHT	
HEARING	
SMELL	
TASTE	
TOUCH	

Today we are going to spend some time in chapter 7 in the *I Want to Trust You, but I Don't* book. If you haven't already read chapter 7, please do so before you begin.

Most of us love a book or a movie in which the bad guy gets what's coming to him in the end. We love to see justice served, when right wins over wrong.

But that's not always how life is. Too many times people who do wrong seem to get away with it. And this is nothing new. Oh, how I relate to King David when he wrote this over three thousand years ago:

> The LORD is a God who avenges. O God who avenges, shine forth. Rise up, Judge of the earth; pay back to the proud what they deserve.
>
> **PSALM 94:1–2**

When evil seems to triumph, we want God to move with swift justice. We'd kind of like to see that justice play out in a way that our offender realizes how much they've hurt us and makes right the wrongs done to us. But what about when justice seems to be delayed or non-existent for those who've done wrong things?

1. Think about an area in your life, or in our world in general, that feels unfair. If you could make a change to right a wrong, what would you do?

King David thought these things too. In fact, the psalms are filled with David's laments over what seemed like God's inaction and are clear that David wanted his offenders to suffer. And yet, he also found a way to acknowledge God's fairness and reassert his faith. It's such a great model for honesty that leads our hearts back into alignment with what we believe to be true about God.

Psalm 139 gives us an interesting reflection into how David balanced his trust in God with his desire for God to address wickedness. Read Psalm 139:17–24 and then answer the following questions.

2. The Hebrew word translated as "thoughts" is the word *rea,* which refers to someone's purpose or intentions. God's thoughts are His plans. In light of that, what do verses 17–18 tell us about David's trust in God?

3. Verses 19–22 take a shift toward David's enemies who were trying to kill him. What have these people done?

4. After acknowledging his anger at wrongdoing, how does David end this psalm? What does it show us about David's heart?

A longing for justice seems to be inherent in our makeup. We often act in ways that we think will bring about justice because a lack of fairness can be so frustrating. Read the quote from the book below, and then answer the following questions.

> "... constantly thinking about what God doesn't seem to be doing, and about my desire for my version of justice to come about, can become an unhealthy focus. This focus, over time, can become an obsession, which if left unattended, can become a stronghold for the enemy of my soul."
>
> (p. 115)

5. We all have our own version of justice; unfortunately, it's skewed because of our humanness. Let's look at a few Bible verses to see what God says about justice. Read each verse and identify important components of God's justice.

Psalm 89:14

Romans 2:11

Jeremiah 22:3

James 2:13

Isaiah 1:17

So often we think of justice as punishment for wrongdoing. But there's another aspect of justice: the distribution of blessings or benefits. We see God show kind justice for the fatherless, widows, and sojourners (Deuteronomy 10:18), for the righteous (Hosea 10:12), and for those who wait on Him (Isaiah 30:18).

Jesus came to bring justice to the poor, the sick, and the outcast. He gave them dignity, value, and love. His every action brought balance back into the lives of those who had been overlooked, rejected, and oppressed.

6. The Beatitudes, found in Matthew 5:1–12, give us an image of how God sees justice. Read this passage with the idea of God's justice in mind. Make a list of the benefits for those who have suffered and who seek to walk in sync with the ways of God.

When we read the Beatitudes, we can almost hear an echo back to the prophecy of the Messiah found in Isaiah 61:1–3.

7. Read Isaiah 61:1–3. What hope does this passage bring to your heart today in your specific situation?

8. God is always balancing the scales of justice because it is in His nature to do so. If we become consumed with a desire to see wrongs punished, we might miss how God is actively righting the wrongs done to us by bringing good to our lives. When you think about being the recipient of a blessing, how can you see God bringing this kind of justice into your life?

9. Even though my head tells me that God is actively working on my behalf, sometimes my heart is slow to believe it. On those days, it helps me to get out into nature and see evidence of Him working in creation.

How do you experience God in nature? What is your favorite place to go to experience Him? Why is that place meaningful to you?

10. Read the following verses and identify how God is working in the world.

   Psalm 19:1

   Romans 1:20

   Colossians 1:16–17

   Acts 14:17

As I said, sometimes my head and heart aren't in alignment when I'm in an unfair situation. Especially when it looks like people are getting away with their hurtful choices. It's in those times when I need to make sure I don't get lured into sinful choices trying to right the wrong. Sometimes those sinful choices are in how I'm thinking.

Please read this book excerpt and answer the questions that follow.

> "I'm tempted to celebrate when those who have caused destruction and devastation experience hardships I think they deserve. But I need to remember that adding more hate and hurt never healed anyone, and it isn't wise. It certainly wouldn't help me find peace. James 3:13–18 teaches us there is wisdom that comes down from above, but there is also another kind of earthly 'wisdom' that can be unspiritual and demonic." (p. 123)

11. Read James 3:13–18 and identify some wrong thinking that is unspiritual. What are the consequences of that thinking?

12. List the aspects of godly wisdom. What are the benefits of that wisdom?

13. Have you seen a situation where there was jealousy and selfish ambition? What kind of disorder and vile practices resulted from that dynamic?

Keeping my heart in a right posture helps me avoid straying into sin. The bottom line is I can trust that God won't leave sin unaddressed. I'm so glad I can trust Him to do so because He is a merciful God. And we always want God's mercy to be in play because we need it too.

As we wrap up this day, I want to remind you of this quote from the book:

> "I pray we cling to this truth today: darkness, sin, and hopelessness have been overcome. Jesus did it for me. And He did it for you. Jesus loves you. Jesus sees you. The battle you're facing, no matter how dark it feels, isn't hopeless. We may not be able to see victory right now, but because of Jesus, evil is in the process of being ultimately defeated." (p. 126)

Spend some time in prayer, thanking God for His unchanging nature and for our ability to trust Him to bring justice as He sees fit.

DAYS 4 & 5

Read chapters 8 and 9.

Use these days to go back and complete any of the reflection questions or activities from the previous days this week that you weren't able to finish. Make note of any revelations you've had and reflect on any growth or personal insights you've gained.

Spend the next two days reading chapters 8 and 9 of the *I Want to Trust You, but I Don't* book. Use the space below to note anything in the chapters that stands out to you or encourages your heart.

Schedule

BEFORE YOUR GROUP GATHERING	Read chapters 8–9 in the *I Want to Trust You, but I Don't* book.
GROUP GATHERING	Watch Video Session 5 Group Discussion Pages 136–146
PERSONAL STUDY DAY 1	Study guide pages 147–152
PERSONAL STUDY DAY 2	Study guide pages 153–159
PERSONAL STUDY DAY 3	Study guide pages 160–165
PERSONAL STUDY DAYS 4 & 5	Read chapter 10 and the Conclusion of the *I Want to Trust You, but I Don't* book.

What If Instead of Controlling, We Decided to Just Wait and See?

WELCOME AND OPENING REFLECTION:
(Suggested time: 15–20 minutes)

Welcome to Session 5 of *I Want to Trust You, but I Don't*.

Leader Note: Before starting the video, take a few moments to check in with your group about how they are doing. Let the group warm up a bit by asking if there was anything from their personal study time they'd like to share with the group.

Another option is to ask this question:

What was a helpful takeaway from chapters 8 and 9 of the book?

VIDEO:
(Run time: 17 minutes)

Leader Note: Play the teaching video for Session 5.

As you watch the video, use the outline below to help you follow along with the teaching and to take additional notes on anything that stands out to you.

Saying "we'll see" doesn't diminish the good. It means we can look at life through the lens of a continuous story rather than isolated instances.

Though we will face unkindness and unfaithfulness in people, hope is not lost because God is kind. God is faithful. When life begs me to believe otherwise, I remind myself that God's not done yet.

The quicker I intentionally recall God's faithfulness in my past, the less I panic and suffer from fear of the future.

Imperfect trust in God's plan is still holy.

Sometimes, God helps us fight battles not with one great big miraculous intervention, but with daily provisions and assurances.

Three important facts about the farmer in the story:

1. He was being responsible, rather than inactive.
2. He had a balanced perspective. He was facing the reality of today without catastrophic thinking about the future.
3. He had a peaceful confidence.

We shouldn't live as if everything is an emergency.

Examples of controlling tendencies:

- Needing to know every detail to ensure you're not caught off guard

- Obsessively trying to figure out how to prevent bad things from happening

- Having an unusual sense that if you take charge of something, you can make things work out

- Assuming others are incapable

- Being overly rigid with boundaries

- Using the silent treatment

- Treating small annoyances as epic offenses

- Looking for opportunities to say, "I told you so"

- Refusing to let others see your vulnerable side so you can stay in charge

Because we know God, we can find peace in His faithful love, justice, and righteousness.

> This is what the LORD says: "Let not the wise boast of their wisdom or the strong boast of their strength or the rich boast of their riches, but let the one who boasts boast about this: that they have the understanding to know me, that I am the LORD, who exercises kindness, justice and righteousness on earth, for in these I delight," declares the LORD.
>
> **JEREMIAH 9:23–24**

Rather than deny our emotions, we can exercise self-control when the anxiety from our more intense feelings makes us want to say and do things we normally wouldn't.

My reaction can mess up my peace. Maturity often comes when we feel discomfort and disappointment and are able to deal with it without falling apart.

Two questions to ask before resorting to controlling tactics:
1. Where is the broken trust stemming from in this situation?
2. Is a person causing this or is this an event God is allowing that I don't understand?

What I can control:

- I can assess to the best of my ability whether or not they are safe.

- I can have healthy conversations with them about my concerns.

- I can determine how closely I let them in and how much access I give them to my heart.

- I can have healthy boundaries that still allow for the relationship to be as close as I deem appropriate.

- I can choose to give my trust to them or not.

We must remember to not transfer our broken trust with humans onto God.

> "God is not human, that he should lie, not a human
> being, that he should change his mind. Does he speak and
> then not act? Does he promise and not fulfill?"
>
> **NUMBERS 23:19**

People can have questionable motives. God does not.

We can't look at isolated instances to determine whether or not God is coming through for us.

Instead of berating God with my suggestions or projections, clenching my fists, and reaching for control, I simply need to embrace the very next thing He shows me. And then the next.

Group Discussion

(SUGGESTED TIME 40–45 MINUTES)

Leader Note: We have included some questions to get your group discussion started. Feel free to add your own or modify what's here. The goal is for your group to have a meaningful discussion.

1. In the video, Lysa told a story about a farmer who chose not to have a panicked response when there was calamity. And who kept times of blessing in perspective as well. Each time, he said, "We'll see." The farmer wisely knew that a bigger story was unfolding.

    Share a time when an incident originally looked negative but turned out to be positive over time.

2. Lysa pointed out that even though life might seem unfair, God is not done. God is always working behind the scenes, and often the work God is doing is changing us. Read the following verses and identify the good work God promises in your life during a hard time.

    2 Corinthians 4:16–18

    2 Corinthians 12:9

1 Peter 1:6–7

James 1:2–4

When we are in the midst of confusing circumstances, when we can't see what God is doing, we can always have a perspective change. With practice, we can exercise discipline to focus on right thoughts and reject wrong thoughts. Paul addressed our thinking in his letter to the Ephesians. Read Ephesians 4:17–24 and then answer the following questions.

3. Paul specifically addresses the way the Gentiles (non-Jews) thought. What does he say about their thinking? (v. 17)

4. How did the Gentiles' thinking become compromised? How can we avoid this same kind of wrong thinking? (vv. 18–19)

5. What were the new believers in Jesus taught to do? (vv. 20–24)

6. Discuss some examples of what it might look like for us to do these same three things:

- Put off our old self

- Be made new in the attitude of our minds

- Put on our new self

7. The farmer in the story displayed a balanced perspective about the good and the bad that happened to him, which meant he wasn't overly optimistic or overly pessimistic about the future. Do you find yourself going in one of these two directions more strongly? If so, how does that way of processing life impact you both in the moment and as time goes along?

8. As we've been discussing in this study, trust is fragile and hard to give. And many of us wish we could put our trust in God more fully. We wish we were people of great faith.

Have someone read Luke 17:5–6.

As you read these verses, you may think to yourselves, *Wait a minute. If I go outside and try to move a tree by faith, will it really move?* We need to ask ourselves this very important question: Is my faith aimed at an outcome or at the goodness of God?

So many times we want to make things happen in our way and in our timing. If things go the way we want them to go, it can feel like our faith accomplished this good outcome. Instead, our focus should be on the goodness of God. We have to trust that God's goodness will be the eventual outcome, even if it's not at all what we want right now. We are trying to make a judgment of whether or not our faith "worked" in one situation. God looks at what needs to happen in the course of time so eventual good will come from even this. In other words, our faith should be in trusting God, not in making the bush move. The exercise of asking a tree to move is symbolic of how important it is to exercise faith in all situations. We may not see the bush move now, but if it is supposed to happen, it will move in the course of time according to God's way.

Rather than thinking the disciples needed more faith or better faith, Jesus seems to be indicating what truly matters is the substance of our faith. What difference does it make for us when we trust in God's goodness rather than the outcome we desire?

9. Read the list of controlling tendencies from the video (listed on page 138) and then discuss some of your experiences with trying to control things.

10. We can all experience anxiety at times through situations and people we can't control. Anxious feelings are normal, and rather than let them dominate our thoughts, we can actually use them as a reminder to reframe those thoughts. Read Jeremiah 9:23–24 from the text below, then answer the following questions.

> This is what the LORD says: "Let not the wise boast of their wisdom or the strong boast of their strength or the rich boast of their riches, but let the one who boasts boast about this: that they have the understanding to know me, that I am the LORD, who exercises kindness, justice and righteousness on earth, for in these I delight," declares the LORD.

What are the dangers of placing our confidence in human wisdom, strength, or wealth instead of in God?

In what areas of your life do you tend to boast or place your confidence? How can you shift your focus to boasting in the Lord?

How can knowing and understanding God more deeply impact the way you live and relate to others?

11. Let's wrap up our time together by reminding ourselves that we may not know why God allows things to happen, but we don't have to be uncertain of His motives. People can have questionable motives. God does not. How does this truth bring you comfort and encouragement for the next week?

CLOSING:

(Suggested time: 5 minutes)

Leader Note: Read the following instructions and clarify any questions your group may have about the homework and what each participant should do between now and the next session. Then, take a few minutes to pray with your group. You can use the prayer provided or pray your own prayer.

BEFORE THE NEXT SESSION . . .

Every week, the *I Want to Trust You, but I Don't Study Guide* includes five days of personal study to help you make meaningful connections between your life and what you're learning each week. This week, you'll do more review of the video we discussed today, and then work through chapters 8 and 9 of the *I Want to Trust You, but I Don't* book. You'll also have time to read chapter 10 and the Conclusion of the book in preparation for our next study together.

PRAYER

Heavenly Father, I confess my tendency to grasp for control and to rely on my own understanding. In my moments of fear, I can easily forget that nothing is outside of Your control. Grant me the courage to release my grip on things and let go of my need to control the outcome. I want to fully surrender my will to Your will. Help me to trust in Your goodness, even when the path ahead seems uncertain. May Your Spirit guide me each step of the way, and may Your will be done in my life. In Jesus' name, Amen.

Personal Study

Today we are going to spend more time reflecting on the Session 5 video in the video series of *I Want to Trust You, but I Don't*. Please take some time to watch that session, if you haven't already.

As I have researched this topic of trust, I've learned that our brains are wired for confidence in knowing. So when things feel unknown or unpredictable, it makes us feel incredibly uncomfortable.

When that happens, we try to produce a temporary confidence in our own abilities. But if we always put confidence in ourselves, things will fall apart because the only safe place to put our confidence is in the Lord.

The story I told in the video about the farmer is such a good reminder that we can make our plans or even try to interpret what happens to us, but in reality, God is the only one in control.

Let's start our day together by remembering this truth from the video:

When life begs me to believe otherwise, I remind myself that God's not done yet. There's more to be revealed.

1. How does this idea bring you comfort today, given the challenging situations in your life or the people you are praying for?

2. Learning to trust God is a process. Part of the process is looking back at our lives and seeing God's faithfulness in the past. This remembrance is an ancient practice that we can apply to our lives today. Think about your life and list three ways the Lord has been faithful to you.

   1)

   2)

   3)

3. We can also be reminded of God's faithfulness through the experiences of others. Read Psalm 145:4–7. Based on these verses, list some ways you can remind yourself of God's faithfulness.

4. There's so much about the farmer in the story that I admire. I'll admit I haven't always had such a calm perspective on life. As I thought about that story, I realized there were three different ways the farmer approached his life. Look at the three qualities the farmer displayed, and identify which one of these perspectives would help you the most today and why.

   - He was being responsible, rather than inactive.

   - He had a balanced perspective. He was facing the reality of today without catastrophic thinking about the future.

   - He had a peaceful confidence.

5. Though the farmer was responsible, he didn't try to control his circumstances. This can be hard for us as humans because we were created to steward the things God gave us. The problem is when we try to control things we were never meant to control. The prophet Jeremiah had some wise words about control. Read Jeremiah 10:23. Summarize this verse in your own words.

6. In the video I listed some examples of controlling tendencies. Review the list and put a check mark by the ones you have experienced in your own life.

    ☐ Needing to know every detail to ensure you're not caught off guard

    ☐ Obsessively trying to figure out how to prevent bad things from happening

    ☐ Having an unusual sense that if you take charge of something, you can make things work out

    ☐ Assuming others are incapable

    ☐ Being overly rigid with boundaries

    ☐ Using the silent treatment

    ☐ Treating small annoyances as epic offenses

    ☐ Looking for opportunities to say, "I told you so"

    ☐ Refusing to let others see your vulnerable side so you can stay in charge

7. When you respond with one of these controlling tendencies, what are you really trying to control? (For example, if you need to know every detail, you may be trying to control the future.)

8. What if you didn't respond to a situation you have faced in the past or are currently facing by trying to control the outcome? What good might have happened?

9. Jesus is our perfect model of someone who didn't try to control His situation. Because His trust in God was complete, He didn't need to manipulate circumstances or people. Instead, Jesus stayed focused on the task before Him. Read the following verses and identify how Jesus responded.

   Matthew 4:1–4

   Luke 10:22–24

   John 5:19

   Matthew 26:39

10. When we can't control things, unchecked emotions can cloud our judgment and we may find ourselves saying or doing things we wouldn't normally do. Rather than deny our emotions, through God's Spirit, we have the power to process them while exercising self-control. Feelings are indicators that something needs to be addressed, but they should never be dictators of how we act and react. What is one area of your life where you are able to show strong self-control? What practices or habits do you have in that area that you could apply when life gets challenging?

11. Reflect on the quote from the video teaching and then answer the following prompt.

> "What if we started looking at the pitfalls in this journey as ways to gain more strength rather than letting hard times steal our strength?"

List some of the ways you've grown stronger through facing hard times.

12. We can make progress in this issue of trying to control others and situations. A big step forward is when we start to accept what's right in front of us—both good and bad. It may be hard at first, but what if we started seeing today as a gift? Waking up today is such rich evidence of God's faithfulness. This day is part of the answer to all the many prayers we've prayed.

What are you experiencing today that is an answer to your prayers in the past?

13. Sometimes we can get so hyperfocused on what God hasn't done that we forget to intentionally call out what He has done. Consider the difference it could make in the way you face today if one of the first things you declare is this:

"I am living out answered prayers right now, this day. Here's how . . ."

Today we are going to work through some of the concepts found in chapter 8 in the *I Want to Trust You, but I Don't* book. If you haven't already read chapter 8, please do so before you begin.

Control is sneaky. We can easily dismiss it as not a problem for us, because we don't fit the stereotype in our minds. After all, we might rationalize, we aren't bossy or demanding. Surely, it's obvious when someone has control issues . . . right?

But have you ever intervened in a situation that didn't involve you to protect a friend or family member from potential pain? Have you ever turned down a good opportunity for your child because you were afraid? Have you ever thought of a plan to get another adult to change or make different choices, even when that person has shown you many times they are unwilling?

If you answered yes, then let me just say: *Me too!*

This is why control can be hard to identify. At times it looks like we are just being responsible. Other times it looks like we are being wise. But sometimes underneath all those seemingly good choices can be a root of control.

1. Let's start our time together by considering what control might look like for you. Think of one situation in which you made a decision or choice that, in hindsight, was rooted in your desire to control the outcome.

2. The more I try to control what isn't my responsibility, the more I feel an underlying anxiety. Maybe you've felt this way, too, when you are trying to hold it all together for the people you love but feeling like you're on the edge of burnout a lot of the time. We can find ourselves in this situation when controlling tendencies sneak their way into our lives.

Yesterday, you looked at a list of controlling behaviors I mentioned in the video. I've added a few more today to help us get a broader sense of what controlling behavior might look like. Review this list and put a check next to the ones you have seen in yourself.

- ☐ Going to unusual lengths to ensure you're not caught off guard
- ☐ Getting annoyed when people deviate from your plan
- ☐ Having unrealistic expectations of others
- ☐ Assuming others are incapable
- ☐ Overplanning
- ☐ Thinking your way is the best way
- ☐ Resorting to guilt-tripping
- ☐ Having a bad attitude when asked to be flexible
- ☐ Recruiting others to put pressure on the one you feel isn't cooperating with your plan

3. Let's get a full picture of what control might look like in your life. Go back and review your responses to the first part of the list (on page 149) and write those down here.

4. Remember, just because we have controlling issues doesn't mean we should label ourselves as controlling. I don't like labels because we can so easily own these to the point that we make them a negative part of our identity. We want to look at these issues so we can work on them, grow, and develop. Now that your potential controlling issues are in one place, which ones do you experience the most often? What are the common things you are trying to control?

The Bible gives us an example of a woman who chose to control a situation rather than trust God's promises. We are first introduced to her as Sarai at the beginning of her story, which is found in the book of Genesis. Let's see what we can learn about the consequences of controlling rather than trusting.

5. Abram, Sarai's husband, was seventy-five years old when God called him to leave his land and go to a new land where God would make him into "a great nation" (Genesis 12:2). Abram obeyed, but with no children, Abram wondered how this nation would come to be. Then, God gave Abram a specific promise. Read Genesis 15:2–5. What was that promise?

6. Though God gave Abram a promise, Sarai, his wife, didn't believe she would conceive a child. Read Genesis 16:1–4a. Why did Sarai take matters into her own hands rather than trust God's timing?

7. Read Genesis 16:4a–6. What were the consequences of Sarai's choices?

8. Even though Sarai made a choice that exposed her distrust in God, God still kept His promise. God established a covenant between Abram and his descendants and changed his name to Abraham and Sarai's name to Sarah. And God reminded Abraham of His promise. Read Genesis 17:17–19. What specifically did God say?

9. On the surface, Sarah lacked faith, but we read something astonishing about her in the New Testament when the author of Hebrews lists the heroes of the faith. Read Hebrews 11:11, and identify the first woman mentioned and what she did to receive this honor.

10. God saw Sarah's faith and credited it to her. What does Sarah's story tell us about God's redemption and restoration even when we make controlling choices that have problematic outcomes?

11. Reflect on this quote from the book and then answer the following questions.

> "Humans who break our trust do not have the power to break apart God's good plans for our lives. They may have enough influence in our lives to hurt our hearts and make us feel derailed. We may even think their actions have created so much destruction that life will never be normal again. But people are never more powerful than God." (p. 140)

It's important to remember that though situations and relationships may look bleak, there is *nothing* God cannot change. What do the following verses tell us about God's authority?

Job 42:2

Psalm 33:10–11

Psalm 115:3, 9–11

Matthew 19:26

12. While there will always be gaps in the trustworthiness of people, there are no gaps
with God. Read Lamentations 3:22–23 and write next to each phrase your thoughts
about what this means to you.

"THE STEADFAST LOVE OF THE Lord NEVER CEASES;	
HIS MERCIES NEVER COME TO AN END;	
THEY ARE NEW EVERY MORNING;	
GREAT IS YOUR FAITHFULNESS."	

13. As I said in the opening of this day's study, control is sneaky. It seems like a way to eliminate stress, but it actually has the opposite effect. Every time we take over, we are telling God that we don't need Him. I'm pretty sure we would agree that we desperately need God's help. The apostle Paul suffered from something he called "a thorn in his flesh." He pleaded for God to remove it from his life, but God didn't. Read 2 Corinthians 12:5–10 and summarize the promise God gives to us.

14. One way to quiet the angst of control is a practice called *surrender*. This doesn't mean we do nothing. It just means we do our job without crossing a line of also trying to do God's job. As we surrender to God the things we don't understand and can't control, the more we will receive His peace. In surrendering, we acknowledge that we don't have ultimate control but that we know who does, and then we wait and trust in His response.

    As we finish this day, let's practice surrendering. Think about a situation you are trying to control (or wish you could control) but feel helpless. If you are ready to surrender that situation, emotion, or action to God, then use the templates below to identify what you are choosing to surrender. Then write what you will choose to do instead. I've given you two places to fill out here, but use this template in your journal or wherever else you want to remember this commitment:

    God, I'm surrendering this _____

    _____

    Instead of _____

    _____

    I'm going to _____

    _____

God, I'm surrendering this _____

_____

Instead of _____

_____

I'm going to _____

_____

Often we struggle with taking back today what we surrendered yesterday. But let's remind ourselves that surrendering is a process. We can celebrate that we're making progress, and then move forward, knowing that imperfect trust is still holy.

Today we are going to work through some of the concepts found in chapter 9 in the I Want to Trust You, but I Don't *book. If you haven't already read chapter 9, please do so before you begin.*

When your trust has been broken, it can feel like life comes to a screeching halt. Working to repair broken trust is full of ups and downs. And if repair doesn't work, it can feel like such a setback or possibly even walking backward. You *want* to make progress, and on some days, you even believe you are making progress. But in the quiet places of your heart, moving forward from relational trauma seems daunting and slow.

It may also seem that everything has been taken from you . . . the person you were, the potential you have, the safety you felt . . . but it hasn't been. The *you* God designed in His image is still there!

1. Let's start today's study with a reminder of all the seeds of potential that God has planted inside you. List some of the things that make you unique. This might be a strength in your thinking or an ability.

Broken trust has a limiting effect. We can easily limit ourselves as a result of another person's actions because past loss overshadows our future. As we've studied, there is nothing another human can do to us that can change God's plans for us. Psalm 118 is a beautiful picture of our potential with God. Read this chapter and answer the following questions.

2. When we wonder if God has forgotten us, what does this passage teach us about God's character?

3. When we wonder if God is ignoring our pain, what does this passage teach us about God's care for us?

4. When we feel helpless, what does this chapter teach us about our strength?

5. When we think no good thing has come our way, what does this passage say about God's blessings?

6. As we've mentioned already in the study, God designed our bodies and minds to heal. As with any injury, sometimes we need help with the healing. The same is true with trauma. Part of healthy processing is a strong support system. What does a healthy support system look like for you? What elements of a support system do you have? What do you need?

7. One thing I learned as part of my healing journey was that unhealed trauma attracts unhealed trauma. The Bible gives us good advice about how to choose healthy relationships and what to avoid. Read the following verses and identify guidelines for what to look for in healthy relationships.

Proverbs 11:3

Ephesians 4:29

Ephesians 5:15–21

Colossians 3:5–17

Proverbs 16:28–3

8. Read the excerpt from the book, then answer answer the questions that follow.

> "Two words that indicated stuck-ness to me were can't and don't . . . If we don't tend well to this kind of broken processing, our can'ts and don'ts will turn into won'ts." (p. 162)

Feeling stuck is such a normal part of getting through trauma. But we don't have to stay stuck. For me, it started with identifying some of the things I believed I couldn't do. Take some time here to identify some of your can'ts and don'ts:

I can't _____

_____

I can't _____

_____

I can't _____

_____

I don't _____

_____

I don't _____

_____

I don't _____

_____

Each of these examples is an opportunity to try something different and to build your resilience muscles. Can you rewrite some of these statements using words that speak a different future? One of possibility? Pick a few and rewrite the sentences into positive statements.

I can _____

_____

I can _____

_____

I will _____

_____

I will _____

_____

9. My soul is prone to freaking out and leaving a place of rest when hard situations arise. But when I read Psalm 116, I see how David wisely processed his concerns, his feelings of oppression, and his alarm. David reframed his panic by returning to the truth he knew about God.

   Take some time to read Psalm 116 now.

As you read this chapter, it could be easy to overlook the focal point of this psalm because it's actually found in the center. This is a Hebrew poetic literary device called a *chiasm*. The structure of the chiasm places the focal point at the center parallel ideas corresponding to each other but all anchored at the center. The pattern can look like A-B-C-B-A. With that understanding, let's look more closely at this psalm.

What is David seeing in his place of alarm?

What was David's response when he focused on the Lord? (vv. 5–6, 7)

What was David's response when he focused on himself? (vv. 10–11)

10. As we look at making progress with trusting others, ourselves, and God, it will feel risky. There may be times when you wonder if you have what it takes. May I be that friend who speaks words of belief over you right now? You are strong enough and brave enough to face hard things, even when you don't know the outcome. Being brave is not always something you feel. It's something you do.

I believe it's possible for you to trust again. And one day, you will look back and see that God has brought good to you out of all you've been through.

To stir up our faith, let's ponder some verses from Isaiah 61. This is a prophetic section of the Old Testament, referring to Jesus, the Messiah who was promised. This was only a future hope for the hearers of Isaiah, but we are now the recipients of this promise. Read Isaiah 61:1–3. What gives you hope from these verses? What gives you comfort? What good does God's Word promise to you?

DAYS 4 & 5

Read chapter 10 and the Conclusion.

Use these days to go back and complete any of the reflection questions or activities from the previous days this week that you weren't able to finish. Make note of any revelations you've had and reflect on any growth or personal insights you've gained.

Spend the next two days reading chapter 10 and the Conclusion of the *I Want to Trust You, but I Don't* book. Use the space below to note anything that stands out to you or encourages your heart.

Schedule

BEFORE YOUR GROUP GATHERING	Read chapter 10 and the Conclusion of the *I Want to Trust You, but I Don't* book.
GROUP GATHERING	Watch Video Session 6 Group Discussion Pages 168–177
PERSONAL STUDY DAY 1	Study guide pages 178–183
PERSONAL STUDY DAY 2	Study guide pages 184–188
PERSONAL STUDY DAY 3	Study guide pages 189–193
PERSONAL STUDY DAYS 4 & 5	Complete any unfinished personal study activities

What Is the Source of My Discernment?

WELCOME AND OPENING REFLECTION:
(Suggested time: 15–20 minutes)

Welcome to Session 6 of *I Want to Trust You, but I Don't.*

Leader Note: Before starting the video, take a few moments to check in with your group about how they are doing. Since this is the last session of this study, ask group members to share any insights they've gained from the study as a whole.

Another option is to answer this question:

What was a helpful takeaway from chapter 10 and the Conclusion of the book?

VIDEO:
(Run time: 19 minutes)

Leader Note: Play the teaching video for Session 6.

As you watch the video, use the outline below to help you follow along with the teaching and to take additional notes on anything that stands out to you.

Unchecked skepticism can leak into other relationships.

There is a big difference between a gut feeling and authentic discernment from the Holy Spirit.

We don't want to immediately assume what we are feeling is "discernment" without checking the source.

When we are feeling skeptical of others, sometimes our feelings are driven by fear, not wisdom.

Just because things feel like reality doesn't mean it is *the* reality.

When feelings are intense we can operate in a self-reliant protective mode more than trusting God to lead us.

Sometimes we need to work on disconnecting our discernment from our extreme fears and reconnecting it to the Holy Spirit.

The source of our discernment is crucial.

Discernment is what fills in the gaps between the facts so we can make more informed decisions.

If we want truth, the source from which that truth comes from matters immensely.

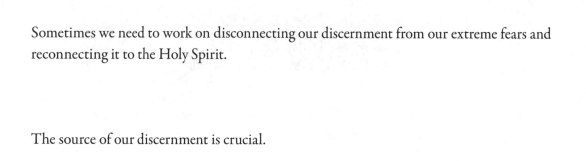

> But the wisdom that comes from heaven is first of all pure; then peace-loving, considerate, submissive, full of mercy and good fruit, impartial and sincere.
>
> **JAMES 3:17**

We need to let God's Word be the guide to wisdom so we can have better discernment.

The worst betrayal I've experienced was when I betrayed myself by not listening to that deep-down knowing that I can now see was the Lord warning me.

"We have two assurances in Scripture: suffering and the presence of the Holy Spirit." —Ann Voskamp (personal conversation)

When we shift from reliance on God to becoming self-reliant, some of these characteristics might emerge:

- Long-term mental fatigue
- Reading God's Word to validate what you're feeling as true rather than reading what is true and letting it guide what you may be feeling
- Isolation by cutting out other godly voices and biblically wise influences that may challenge your thinking
- Constantly looking for signs or proof that will move your own agenda further
- Rejecting the facts of a situation because you've already decided your truth is *the* truth
- Assigning narratives to people that they've never said or motives they don't have
- Spending more time fretting about worries and fears than intentionally focusing on God's wisdom
- Becoming so convinced that you are right that you justify treating anyone who opposes you in rude, harsh, and often demeaning ways

> So I say, walk by the Spirit, and you will not gratify the desires
> of the flesh. For the flesh desires what is contrary to the Spirit,
> and the Spirit what is contrary to the flesh. They are in conflict
> with each other, so that you are not to do whatever you want.
> But if you are led by the Spirit, you are not under the law . . .
> Since we live by the Spirit, let us keep in step with the Spirit.
>
> **GALATIANS 5:16–18, 25**

Three ways to live in light of the Holy Spirit

- Walk by the Spirit (external status)—This is your actions toward others.
- Be led by the Spirit (internal status)—This is your thinking and how you process internally.
- Keep in step with the Spirit (the proximity between you and the Spirit)—This is your daily desire.

Walking by the Spirit, being led by the Spirit, and keeping in step with the Spirit mean you are positioning yourself to receive godly guidance.

We want God's voice to be louder than our fears, other people's opinions, our own agendas, and our doubts.

Group Discussion

(SUGGESTED TIME 40–45 MINUTES)

Leader Note: We have included some questions to get your group discussion started. Feel free to add your own or modify what's here. The goal is for your group to have a meaningful discussion.

1. In our last session together, we will discuss the God-given gift of discernment. When you hear the word "discernment," what are some ideas you had about it before starting this study?

2. God gives us different kinds of discernment. We gain discernment through life experiences, we can draw on biblical principles by relying on godly friends and their perspectives, and finally, we are given supernatural wisdom. Read the following Bible passages and identify which type of discernment is represented in each.

    Hebrews 4:12

    Hebrews 5:14

    Proverbs 15:22

1 Corinthians 2:15–16

1 Thessalonians 5:19–22

John 16:13

3. Discernment goes hand in hand with wisdom. Most often we find wisdom helping us navigate everyday issues, but discernment guides us in distinguishing good from evil. From what we learned in the video and the book, discuss how wisdom and discernment might differ, and how they can work together.

4. Read James 3:17. The source of our wisdom impacts our discernment, which then impacts the health or harm of our decision-making. What does this verse say about the wisdom that comes from God? What might that look like as we grow in wisdom and practice discernment?

5. When we are learning discernment, it can start as a simple nudge to our hearts or a thought about a person or situation. But because of past trauma, it's important to distinguish the source of that nudge. Because we are human, our emotions will always play a part in our discernment. Look at the two verses listed below and discuss how being aware of our human responses can actually help us grow in discernment.

    Jeremiah 17:9

    James 1:5–7

6. Growing in any gift of the Holy Spirit is a process. We receive our spiritual gifts in seed form, and it's our job to cultivate them. Read Hebrews 5:14 again, but this time, discuss what kinds of practice might be helpful to grow discernment in our lives.

7. In the video, Lysa said that the worst betrayal she experienced was when she betrayed herself by not listening to that deep-down knowing. Share some reasons why we might ignore what feels like the Holy Spirit warning us.

8. Even though God has offered us so much discernment and wisdom, we so often turn back to self-reliance. This is a place of comfort for us. But over time, as we depend on ourselves more than we depend on God, we can find some challenging characteristics develop in our lives. Refer back to the list of potential characteristics on page 171, and share if you've experienced any of these.

9. Read Galatians 5:16–18. Let's look at the three ways we can "keep in step with the Spirit" that are mentioned in the video. If time permits, discuss each of these examples and answer the questions. If you are limited on time, have group members answer one of the questions.

    • Walk by the Spirit: Our outward actions can demonstrate that the Spirit of God is within us. What are some actions that tell other people there is something different about us?

    • Be led by the Spirit: This is our thinking and internal processing. How can we know that our thinking is impacted by the Holy Spirit? What differences do you see?

    • Keep in step with the Spirit: These are our daily desires. Do we find ourselves wanting more of God or more of serving ourselves? Share examples of what keeping in step with the Spirit might look like.

CLOSING:

(Suggested time: 5 minutes)

Leader Note: End your session by reading the "Final Personal Studies" instructions to the group, and clarify any questions your group may have about the final week of this study. Then, take a few minutes to pray with your group. You can use the prayer provided or pray your own prayer.

FINAL PERSONAL STUDIES . . .

Every week, the *I Want to Trust You, but I Don't Study Guide* includes five days of personal study to help you make meaningful connections between your life and what you're learning each week. This week, you'll work with the material in the session 6 video, chapter 10, and the Conclusion of the book. You'll also have some time to review the study as a whole.

PRAYER

Dear Lord, we are so thankful for the gift of Your Holy Spirit. As we face decisions, both big and small, we ask for discernment to distinguish between Your truth and the deceptions of the enemy. Open our eyes to see beyond the surface of whatever situation we are facing. Help us to quiet the fear that can interfere with us hearing from You. Teach us to walk in step with Your Spirit, leaning not on our own understanding but trusting in Your unfailing wisdom. In all things, may Your peace reign in our hearts, anchoring our souls in Your steadfast love and truth. In Jesus' name, Amen.

Personal Study

*Today we are going to reflect on the teaching video for session 6 of
I Want to Trust You, but I Don't. If you haven't already watched the
video, please take some time to do so before you begin.*

Hi friend. Here we are in our final week. We've already learned so much together about processing broken trust.

We've learned about ourselves and the cost to our hearts from betrayal.

We learned about others and what to watch for to keep relationships healthy.

We've learned about the trustworthiness of God and how He is the safest place to attach our trust.

And this week we are learning how God has uniquely equipped us with His Spirit to help us discern what is good and what is harmful. I know we've studied discernment in a previous week, but as I processed all that I've been learning about the Holy Spirit, I felt it was important to understand more and dig a little deeper.

Let's start today by discussing the Holy Spirit before we address discernment.

The Holy Spirit is the third person of the Trinity, including God the Father and Jesus the Son. The Spirit is "through whom God acts, reveals His will, empowers individuals, and discloses His personal presence in the Old Testament and the New Testament."[8]

---

8 Paul Jackson, "Holy Spirit," in *Holman Illustrated Bible Dictionary*, ed. Chad Brand and Eric Mitchell (Nashville: Holman Bible Publisher, 2003), 773.

1. What is your understanding of the role of the Holy Spirit in the life of a believer? Where are some of the places you've learned about the Holy Spirit?

2. Read Ephesians 1:13–14. When does the Bible say we receive the gift of the Holy Spirit?

3. When Jesus was living amongst us on the earth, the Holy Spirit did not indwell believers. Read John 14:25–27. What did Jesus tell His disciples about the Holy Spirit?

4. We learn about the roles of the Holy Spirit in different places in the Bible. As we grow in our knowledge and understanding of how He works in our lives, we also grow in our experience of Him. Read the following passages and identify the work of the Spirit.

   Romans 8:26

   Galatians 5:22–23

   Acts 1:8

   John 16:8

   Luke 12:11–12

Ezekiel 36:26–27

1 Corinthians 12:1–13

5. God gives us discernment for our good, for our protection, and for the good of other believers. But sometimes we confuse our thoughts with God's thoughts. I mentioned that my fears and trauma interfered with my discernment from God. What are some other feelings, thoughts, or emotions that can be the source of your "discernment"?

6. Read 1 Corinthians 2:10b–11a. How does God Himself help us when we are having trouble distinguishing between our thoughts and God's? How does this passage encourage you to increase your godly discernment?

7. Discernment isn't a standalone gift. Read Philippians 1:9–10 and identify how the apostle Paul described what would be needed for the Philippians to be more discerning. What should our hearts be like when we are seeking to discern the truth?

8. As we've studied, God is generous to give us wisdom and discernment. But too often we rely on ourselves more than we rely on God. When we depend on our human discernment over time, we can find ourselves traveling down mental pathways that are exhausting and detrimental. In the video, I shared a list of possible characteristics we might experience. Take some time here to do some personal reflection. If you've experienced the characteristic in the left column, jot down a thought, situation, or person that comes to mind in the right column.

Long-term mental fatigue	
Reading God's Word to validate what you're feeling as true rather than reading what is true and letting it guide what you may be feeling	
Isolation by cutting out other godly voices and biblically wise influences that may challenge your thinking	
Constantly looking for signs or proof that will move your own agenda further	
Rejecting the facts of a situation because you've already decided your truth is the truth	
Assigning narratives to people that they've never said or motives they don't have	
Spending more time fretting about worries and fears than intentionally focusing on God's wisdom	
Becoming so convinced that you are right that you justify treating anyone who opposes you in rude, harsh, and often demeaning ways	

9. The apostle Paul addressed issues among the Christian believers who lived in Galatia. As we are learning in the study, just like we can tend to do, they relied on themselves more than God. But Paul reminded them that they have the Spirit to lead them away from desires of the "flesh" and toward walking in the Spirit. Read Galatians 5:13–18, 25.

- What issue was Paul addressing in verses 13–15? What kind of outward actions might have been happening?

- What is the answer to the ways the Galatians were living?

- Paul indicated that we have two natures: one of the flesh given at our natural birth, and the other given at our spiritual rebirth when we became a Christian. How do you experience this conflict of two opposing natures in your life?

10. Keeping in step with the Spirit is crucial to cultivating the discernment God wants us to have. In the video, I shared three ways to keep in step with the Spirit. In each of these areas, identify one way you can apply this instruction in the coming week.

Walk by the Spirit (visible actions that others can see)

Be led by the Spirit (internal ways of thinking and processing)

Keep in step with the Spirit (monitor your desires toward God or away from Him)

11. Let's end today's study time by reviewing the list of ways we can know we are keeping in step with the Spirit. Our lives will change when we pursue the things of the Spirit over the desires of our human nature. These changes don't happen overnight, but they can happen gradually as we submit our will to God. Like we did in an earlier question today, spend some time processing these examples. If you've experienced the characteristic in the left column, jot down a thought, situation, or person that comes to mind in the right column.

Actions of a Spirit-led person	
Love replaces selfishness	
Joy replaces angry outbursts and edgy frustration	
Peace replaces demands for control	
Patience replaces a quick temper	
Kindness replaces rudeness	
Goodness replaces selfish ambition	
Faithfulness replaces incessant desires for self-gratification	
Gentleness replaces a harsh approach	
Self-control replaces unrestrained impulses	

Today we are going to reflect on chapter 10 in the *I Want to Trust You, but I Don't* book. If you haven't already read chapter 10, please take some time to do so before you begin.

Resiliency is a beautiful quality. It doesn't mean there won't be evidence of what we endured. There might be scars that last a long time. But a resilient person is one who weathers a storm, yet is still growing and thriving.

I believe this is true for you. You have gone through so much. But because you have committed to this study, you are growing. God is working in you every time you open His Word and listen for His voice.

You are preparing for a new season. Isn't that exciting? It won't look like the last one, because we can never go back. And would we even want to?

1. As we start today's study, spend some time thinking about what a new season could look like for you. Write down some of your hopes for the future.

2. The image of the fallen tree with new roots really stuck with me. The tree hadn't lost who it was, but it gained new life by growing new roots. Read Colossians 2:6–7. How can believers in Jesus grow spiritually as we root ourselves in Him?

3. There's another image of growing things that we can apply to our lives. Read John 15:5–8. From what you know about vines and branches, what does dependence on Jesus look like in this passage?

4. Resiliency happens when we don't give up and we seek a healthy path to recovery. The benefit of this work is that the next time a storm happens, we know what to do. We know how to withstand it. The Bible affirms there are other benefits of resilience. Read the following verses and write down the benefits listed.

1 Peter 4:13–16

James 1:12

Hebrews 12:1–3

5. Reflect on the quote from the book and answer the questions that follow.

> "The real solution [for trust issues] is to accept that trust isn't ever a guarantee with humans. Some relationships will hurt us. Some relationships will help heal us. But if we anchor our hope to the Lord, the risks of trust will be much less terrifying as we develop the muscles of resiliency." (pp. 171, 173)

- What are some practical ways we can anchor our hope in the Lord and build resilience in the face of relational challenges?

- We've addressed how resilience helps us, but how can we support others as we develop our resilience muscles?

6. Read this quote from the book and answer the following question.

> "The woman who thrives in life isn't the one who never has her heart broken. It's the one who plants her brokenness in the rich soil of her faith in God and waits with anticipation to see what good thing God will grow next." (p. 173)

Shifting our thoughts from the next possible pain point in life to living in anticipation of what God will do next might feel like a big task. It will require we address our negative thinking and intentionally shift those thoughts to the belief that God will come through for us.

Based on all we've studied in the past five weeks, list some things you believe about God and how He will work in your life in the future.

_____

_____

_____

_____

7. We've learned so much about God through this study, and one thing we can count on is that God is a grower. When He takes His supernatural ability and applies it to our lives, we know there will be multiplication of some kind. As I said in the book, "Nothing we ever place in God's hands will be returned without meaning" (p.173). God can take our "not enough" and make it "more than enough"!

Let's take a look at some examples of how God takes what looks like a problem and turns it around.

- Read John 2:1–11. What did Jesus do in His first recorded miracle? How did Jesus turn that day around?

- Read Matthew 14:13–21. This miracle was so important that all four Gospels record it. How did Jesus change that situation?

- Read 2 Kings 4:1–7. How did God turn not enough into enough?

8. Consider the hard situations and broken trust you have endured. How are you feeling "not enough"? You can list specific examples or relationships that are leading you to feel this way.

9. As you were reading this chapter, did you underline or highlight any sentences or ideas that spoke to you? Go back through this chapter and copy some of the sentences that stood out to you most.

10. I wish I could assure you God will always highlight potentially hurtful people or situations. But that's not the way discernment works. But when we don't know what to do, we have a direct line to God in prayer. If you are feeling confused about a situation or person, and you desire greater discernment, write a prayer to God asking for His help.

Today we are going to reflect on the Conclusion of the *I Want to Trust You, but I Don't* book. If you haven't already read the Conclusion, please take some time to do so before you begin.

We've made it to the end of this study. Thank you for joining me on this journey. I'm so very proud of you for investing time, thought, and prayer into these past six weeks. As we studied yesterday, nothing we put in God's hands ever returns without meaning.

Our trials and suffering are never wasted. We can trust that God will use everything we've experienced at some point in our lives. Either to bless us or to bless someone else.

This is how we find meaning in what we've gone through.

What happened to us, and how God brought us through it, will inspire someone else. That's what happened to me with the blog post I wrote fifteen years before I wrote this book. God used those words to remind me I wasn't alone in what I went through.

Our story is part of the hope that God is creating for someone else. This is such an encouragement to me, and I hope it is for you as well.

1. How does it encourage you today to know that God will use your pain to help someone else?

2. As we've already discussed, God doesn't waste our pain. In fact, one of the paradoxes of our faith is that we experience God's presence and power most intensely in our hard times. The apostle Paul was one of the first followers of Jesus who had many trials and troubles. He had an inspiring perspective. He saw his experiences as a way to encourage other believers in their times of trouble.

Read the following passages in 2 Corinthians and identify the perspective shift Paul calls us to.

2 Corinthians 1:9–10

2 Corinthians 4:17–18

3. Paul also pointed out a way that God intentionally uses our sufferings as a way for us to care for others. Read 2 Corinthians 1:3–5 and list how God uses what happens to us to bless others.

4. As we walk through our own brokenness, let's remind ourselves that there are some certainties we can count on as believers. We can still count on truth, grace, joy, and beauty. Read the following passages and capture your thoughts about these timeless truths.

Truth

John 14:6

1 John 4:9

John 8:31–32

Grace

Ephesians 2:8–9

Hebrews 4:16

Romans 5:6

Joy

Romans 14:17

John 16:22

1 Peter 1:8

Beauty

Psalm 27:4

Isaiah 28:5–6

Ecclesiastes 3:11

5. We have so much to be thankful for. The Bible calls us to have a heart of gratitude, and as we approach the end of this study, it feels right to spend some time listing the things God has done for us. This could be through this study, or as you look at your past. Make a list of ten things you are thankful for today, and then thank and praise God for His goodness to you.

> Give thanks to the LORD, for he is good; his love endures forever.
>
> **PSALM 107:1**

1.

2.

3.

4.

5.

6.

7.

8.

9.

10.

6. To end our time together, I'd like to invite you to look back at the poem I shared in my book on pages 174–175 of what healing and trusting look like. Now it's your time to record some of your own thoughts. You've come so far. You've experienced healing. Your future is full of possibility. Let's celebrate the work God has done in your life as our final declaration that in Christ, we have the victory!

HEALING LOOKS LIKE	TRUSTING AGAIN LOOKS LIKE

DAYS 4 & 5

Use these days to go back and complete any of the reflection questions or activities from the previous days this week that you weren't able to finish. Make note of any revelations you've had and reflect on any growth or personal insights you've gained.

Leader's Guide

Thanks for choosing the *I Want to Trust You, but I Don't* video Bible study. Please take a few minutes to read this helpful information before you begin. It should answer most questions you may have.

WHAT MATERIALS ARE NEEDED FOR A SUCCESSFUL GROUP?

- ☐ Television monitor or screen
- ☐ DVD player or device for video streaming
- ☐ Six-session video series with author Lysa TerKeurst
- ☐ Watch or clock with which to monitor time
- ☐ One study guide for each group member (they will be writing in the study guide, so they will each need a copy)
- ☐ One copy of the book *I Want to Trust You, but I Don't* for each group member (they will be reading the book between meetings, so they will each need a copy)
- ☐ Bible(s)
- ☐ Pen or pencil for each person

HOW DO I PREPARE BEFORE THE GROUP MEETS?

This video Bible study can work equally well in church and home groups. It is designed to adapt to group meetings of 90–120 minutes in length. The first thing you need to do is determine how much time your group has available to meet. Then look at the session outline for the group you will be leading. The outline shows suggested times for each section of the study, based on a 90-minute meeting (video times are exact; others are approximates). Depending on your group's specified meeting times, you can decide how you want to allocate your discussion and optional activity engagement.

If you have a group with limited time to meet each week, you can devote two meetings to each session in the study guide. In the second meeting, you can spend the time normally devoted to watching the video to discuss what you got out of the personal study and your reading of the book.

Viewing the video before your group meets will help you know what to expect and select the questions for the study guide you want to include.

Make sure the room where you are viewing the video has chairs arranged so that everyone can see the screen. When it is time for group discussion, you may need to move chairs so that people in each discussion circle are facing each other. If your whole group will be discussing the material together, having chairs in a semicircle usually allows everyone to see the screen and one another's faces. If your group is large, we recommend that people divide into discussion circles of four to six people; arrange chairs accordingly.

Participants should read the introduction and chapter 1 of the *I Want to Trust You, but I Don't* book before the first meeting and video teaching. Prior to each session in the study guide is a schedule of what participants can expect during the coming week. Please be sure to remind group members which chapters to read each week to prepare for the next teaching video. At the end of each personal study time in the study guide these instructions are repeated.

For some people, this study will be exactly what they need to walk them through a hard season or help them process a deep hurt. For others, this might only be the starting place for their healing. Please know there are some difficult realities that only a licensed Christian counselor will be able to help them navigate. At no point in this study should you ever feel the pressure to be someone's counselor. Below are some resources you can share with anyone in your group who is needing extra help.

FINDING A COUNSELOR:

American Association of Christian Counselors: www.aacc.net
Focus on the Family: www.focusonthefamily.com

THE THERAPY & THEOLOGY PODCAST

Lysa TerKeurst created a podcast with her personal, licensed professional counselor Jim Cress, as well as Proverbs 31 Ministries director of theology, Dr. Joel Muddamalle, that addresses topics such as boundaries, forgiveness, reconciliation, divorce, anxiety, and narcissism.

You can find all of these episodes wherever you listen to podcasts, on the official Proverbs 31 Ministries YouTube channel, or at Proverbs31.org.

GROUP SESSION 1

The Requirements for Trust

Please have group members read the introduction and chapter 1 of *I Want to Trust You, but I Don't* before this meeting.

As the leader, personally view the video before your group meets, and review the discussion questions in the study guide to prepare according to your group's time constraints.

Session Outline

Welcome and Opening Reflection (15–20 minutes)
Watch Video (24 minutes)
Group Discussion (40–45 minutes)
Closing (5 minutes)

GROUP SESSION 2

Do They Value Trust Like You Do?

Please have group members read chapters 2 and 3 of the *I Want to Trust You, but I Don't* book before this meeting.

As the leader, personally view the video before your group meets, and go through the session in the study guide to choose the questions you want to cover.

Session Outline

Welcome and Opening Reflection (15–20 minutes)
Watch Video (18 minutes)
Group Discussion (40–45 minutes)

Closing (5 minutes)

GROUP SESSION 3

Trust Is a Track Record

Please have group members read chapters 4 and 5 of the *I Want to Trust You, but I Don't* book before this meeting.

As the leader, personally view the video before your group meets, and go through the session in the study guide to choose the questions you want to cover.

Session Outline

Welcome and Opening Reflection (15–20 minutes)
Watch Video (15 minutes)
Group Discussion (40–45 minutes)
Closing (5 minutes)

GROUP SESSION 4

The More I Doubt Him, the Less I'll Trust Him

Please have group members read chapters 6 and 7 of the *I Want to Trust You, but I Don't* book before this meeting.

As the leader, personally view the video before your group meets, and go through the session in the study guide to choose the questions you want to cover.

Session Outline

Welcome and Opening Reflection (15–20 minutes)
Watch Video (20 minutes)
Group Discussion (40–45 minutes)
Closing (5 minutes)

GROUP SESSION 5

What if Instead of Controlling, We Decided to Just Wait and See

Please have group members read chapters 8 and 9 of the *I Want to Trust You, but I Don't* book before this meeting.

As the leader, personally view the video before your group meets, and go through the session in the study guide to choose the questions you want to cover.

Session Outline

Welcome and Opening Reflection (15–20 minutes)
Watch Video (17 minutes)
Group Discussion (40–45 minutes)
Closing (5 minutes)

GROUP SESSION 6

What Is the Source of My Discernment?

Please have group members read chapter 10 and the Conclusion of the *I Want to Trust You, but I Don't* book before this meeting.

As the leader, personally view the video before your group meets, and go through the session in the study guide to choose the questions you want to cover.

Session Outline

Welcome and Opening Reflection (15–20 minutes)
Watch Video (19 minutes)
Group Discussion (40–45 minutes)
Closing (5 minutes)

Some Important Notes to Consider on Abuse

A couple of times throughout this book, I've referenced not excusing away abuse or dysfunctional behavior. You know from reading so much about my personal experiences, my heart is very tender and compassionate toward anyone facing destructive relational realities. I wanted to provide this information, both as a point of compassion and clarity around what abuse is and as a way to potentially find help if you're in an abusive situation.

In an article published by *Psychology Today*, I found this definition of abuse:

> Abuse within families is behaviorally nuanced and emotionally complex. Always, it is within a dynamic of power and control that emotional and physical abuse is perpetuated.
>
> Abuse may manifest as physical (*throwing, shoving, grabbing, blocking pathways, slapping, hitting, scratches, bruises, burns, cuts, wounds, broken bones, fractures, damage to organs, permanent injury, or even murder*), sexual (*suggestive flirtatiousness, propositioning, undesired or inappropriate holding, kissing, fondling of sexual parts, oral sex, or any kind of forceful sexual activity*), or emotional (*neglect, harassment, shaming, threatening, malicious tricks, blackmail, unfair punishments, cruel or degrading tasks, confinement, abandonment*).[9]

9 Blake Griffin Edwards, "Secret Dynamics of Emotional, Sexual, and Physical Abuse," *Psychology Today*, February 23, 2019, https://www.psychologytoday.com/us/blog/progress-notes/201902/secret-dynamics-emotional-sexual-and-physical-abuse

So, what does the Bible say about abuse, and what do we do about it? Let's look at what Paul wrote to Timothy:

> But understand this, that in the last days there will come times of difficulty. For people will be lovers of self, lovers of money, proud, arrogant, abusive, disobedient to their parents, ungrateful, unholy, heartless, unappeasable, slanderous, without self-control, brutal, not loving good, treacherous, reckless, swollen with conceit, lovers of pleasure rather than lovers of God, having the appearance of godliness, but denying its power. Avoid such people. (2 Timothy 3:1–5 ESV)

I'm thankful for verses like these that clearly state to avoid abusive people. But how to avoid them and exactly how this is carried out is so very complex. It's impossible to put a broad, sweeping formula on top of hard relationships. There are so many factors that must be sorted out with people trained to recognize danger and to help lead those in abusive situations to know what to do and how to do it.

Here are some things to consider:

- It is good to have wise people speaking into our lives and to process life concerns with godly mentors and trusted friends. Here's a good verse to help discern people of wisdom in your life:

  > Who is wise and understanding among you? By his good conduct let him show his works in the meekness of wisdom. But if you have bitter jealousy and selfish ambition in your hearts, do not boast and be false to the truth. This is not the wisdom that comes down from above, but is earthly, unspiritual, demonic. For where jealousy and selfish ambition exist, there will be disorder and every vile practice. But the wisdom from above is first pure, then peaceable, gentle, open to reason, full of mercy and good fruits, impartial and sincere. And a harvest of righteousness is sown in peace by those who make peace. (James 3:13–18 ESV)

- These trusted friends and godly mentors speaking wisdom into our lives can help us recognize behaviors that cross the line and should be brought to the attention of a professional counselor educated on the issues at hand or, in more urgent situations, to the attention of authorities.

If you need to find a professional Christian counselor in your area, both Focus on the Family and the American Association of Christian Counselors have recommendations listed on their websites, or your church may also have a list of trusted Christian counselors they recommend.

Please know, friend, you are loved, you are not alone, and you don't have to walk through this without help. Remember, the person who is hurting you needs help that only trained professionals can give them. Getting the proper authorities involved isn't being unloving . . . it's actually for your safety and theirs.

About the Author

Photo by Kelsie McGarty

Lysa TerKeurst Adams is president and chief visionary officer of Proverbs 31 Ministries and the author of seven *New York Times* bestsellers, including *Good Boundaries and Goodbyes*, *Forgiving What You Can't Forget*, and *It's Not Supposed to Be This Way*. She enjoys life with her husband, Chaz, and her kids and grandkids. Connect with her at www.LysaTerKeurst.com or on social media @LysaTerKeurst.

Proverbs 31
MINISTRIES

About Proverbs 31 Ministries

Lysa TerKeurst Adams is president and chief visionary officer of Proverbs 31 Ministries.

If you were inspired by *I Want to Trust You, but I Don't* and desire to deepen your own personal relationship with Jesus Christ, we have just what you're looking for.

Proverbs 31 Ministries exists to be a trusted friend who will take you by the hand and walk by your side, leading you one step closer to the heart of God through:

  Free *First 5* Bible study app
  Free online daily devotions
  Circle 31 Book Club
  The Proverbs 31 Ministries Podcast
  Therapy and Theology Podcast
  COMPEL Pro Writers Training
  She Speaks Conference
  Books and resources

Our desire is to help you to know the Truth and live the Truth. Because when you do, it changes everything.

For more information about Proverbs 31 Ministries, visit
www.Proverbs31.org

Also Available

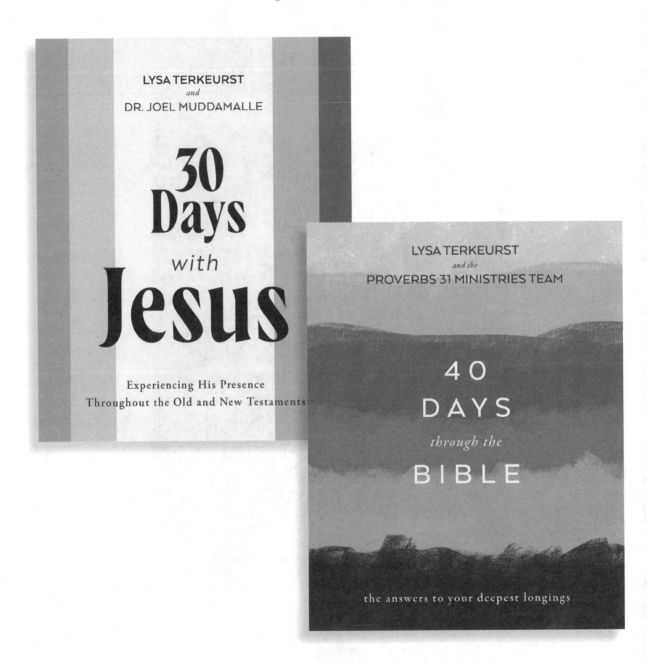

More Video Studies from Lysa TerKeurst

AVAILABLE NOW
and streaming online at
StudyGateway.com

HarperChristian Resources.com